DEEMED NONESSENTIAL

What Happened to Daily Newspapers?

Death of Print from the Internet to the Pandemic

DEEMED NONESSENTIAL

What Happened to Daily Newspapers?

Death of Print from the Internet to the Pandemic

By

ANDY ANDREWS

Bookstand Publishing
www.bookstandpublishing.com

Published by
Bookstand Publishing
Pasadena, CA 91101
4827_4

ISBN 978-1-953710-02-4

Library of Congress Control Number: 2020924324

Dedication

This book would have been impossible to write without my wife, Debbie. Thank you, my love.

Contents

For the Reader

The love readers have for newspapers is precious and everlasting. Many generations, from the great generation to Gen Y, await the delivery of "their" newspaper every morning so they can sit in their preferred chair and, with their favorite beverage, read the news. However, in the past two decades, readers' newspaper "lifestyle" has been threatened.

Increasingly, newsrooms are understaffed. Readership is underserved. The situation was made worse by not only the recession of 2008-2009, but exacerbated — in fact, inflamed — by the "coronavirus recession" of 2020.

What has been destroying newspapers? Like the buggy whip manufacturers of the early 1900s, before the invention of the automobile, will newsrooms become obsolete? Are there ways a community newspaper can survive?

If newspaper offices are to stay open, what is their formula for success?

DEEMED NONESSENTIAL is semi-autobiographical in nature with plenty of anecdotes about my own four-decade-long career in journalism.

I've worked for several major community newspapers, including the Harrisburg *Patriot-News* and the *Reading Eagle*, in addition to a large trade newspaper at LNP Weeklies in Ephrata, Pennsylvania.

I have witnessed massive changes — many that were traumatic to staff and subscribers — to my own beloved industry in four decades of my career.

How did newspapers go from being a powerhouse to the poorhouse? Why did this happen? If they are fortunate to be in operation anymore, newspapers remain in serious jeopardy.

Yet some have stayed successful, despite a Great Recession and a pandemic-induced depression.

In the newspaper field, I have worked on both sides — editorial and advertising. I've always considered myself a hybrid of a working journalist who understands the importance along with the challenges and rewards — of advertising sales.

On a local and national basis, DEEMED NONESSENTIAL examines how newspapers went from pay-for-print to free news to paywall, and how the internet has single-handedly played a critical role in newspapers' demise. I understand the shortfalls by today's journalists, but it's clear why this is happening.

And, as a result of the COVID-19 business and work lockdowns in 2020, why were many journalists suddenly deemed "nonessential" personnel and forced to go on furlough or, worse, lose their jobs?

Have newspapers themselves become "nonessential" in the days of digital subscriptions to websites and push notifications on smartphones?

Will this destroy the lifestyle that newspaper readers have enjoyed for decades?

Will print presses stop for good?

As a newspaperman, I have experienced the decline of an industry that stretches back in time, into the early 1990s. However, during the '70s and '80s, and at least until the mid-'90s, newspapers went from absolutely essential to absurdly extinguished. Page counts by section went from the 40s down to the 10s.

What caused their collapse? At one time, to stem the collapse of subscribers — or simply to build a better subscriber base — many newspapers decided to post free copy on their websites. Was this a good idea? Or did it backfire and alienate readers?

Who are the readers of this book? It's for those who not only love newspapers and rely on them, but for those who have made a living in print journalism and who know friends and relatives who do. I will reminisce about better days. Oh, there were plenty of better days. What has happened to newspapers? What caused the decline?

What is happening? Newspaper readership and advertising are collapsing. Disruptions were caused especially and maybe all because of the internet. Blame Google, Bing and Facebook for much of the demise. In DEEMED NONESSENTIAL, I will explain how that happened and why.

Where did all this occur? Throughout the country, in every state, newspaper staffing and readership has declined in record numbers. Pennsylvania remains a microcosm for the nation and the world.

When did all this happen? DEEMED NONESSENTIAL examines the past to connect the dots to the present-day.

Newspapers were king through the late 1970s until 2000. What has happened to community news since?

Why did I write this book? I wanted to explain the grief that readers and journalists have had in this industry for at least the past two decades. DEEMED NONESSENTIAL provides a look back on four decades of print journalism. What happened to the presses? Ultimately, what happened to scores of journalists who are looking for work elsewhere or forced to pursue other lines of work?

How was this information compiled? Through a series of look-backs on my own career coupled with what was happening in the industry from the late 1970s until now. I believe I have captured the opinions of many sources in the industry, including actual newspaper managing editors, in DEEMED NONESSENTIAL. And I look into my own recent COVID-19 layoff from a media conglomerate.

Introduction

WHAT WENT WRONG?

What has happened to the daily newspaper? How did it go from being the kingpin of news dissemination to a thin section of newsprint sitting on a shelf near the grocery store checkout aisle?

When, and why, did the newspaper go from being the singular most essential tool for the spread of information to be replaced by text on a smartphone you hold in your hand?

And how many journalists, since the fall of print newspapers, have taken an economic hit and have been deemed "nonessential"?

This book looks back 40 years to the reasons newspapers have fallen out of favor and lost subscribers as well as advertisers. Semi-autobiographical in nature, there is enough of my own experience with nearly four decades of publication employment, including working for two daily newspapers and one weekly, in addition to specialty monthly publications, to connect the dots from how great they once were to what they have become: investment engines and market grabs for media conglomerates. While this book, for the most part, is anecdotal, I provide a history of the newspaper industry — at least in southeast Pennsylvania — to reflect what has been going on nationwide.

In earlier chapters, I try to provide some answers. How did newspapers get this way? What were the instruments created long ago to create the near-demise of print journalism?

In later chapters, I try to answer this question: What happened to newspaper revenue?

And what happened to those who were "deemed nonessential"? Many were furloughed, especially in sales. Many had their positions eliminated, such as yours truly. It didn't matter how devoted to your work or dedicated to your career and the business you were in: the sharp economic downturn as a result of businesses shutting down in many states, especially in Pennsylvania during the lockdown from late March to August 2020, had devastating effects.

Restaurants and bars closed, some for good. Retailers cut back on staff, some permanently. Essential businesses sent people to work from home. Some of those who were lucky enough to have a secure job were ordered to work from home, many permanently.

How bad has the COVID-19 pandemic been to the newspaper industry?

Let's look at the numbers:

According to journalism.org, total estimated advertising revenue for the newspaper industry in 2018 was $14.3 billion, based on analysis of financial statements for publicly traded newspaper companies. This is down 13% from 2017. Total estimated circulation revenue was $11.0 billion, compared with $11.2 billion in 2017.

For newspaper ad revenue, according to journalism.org, the best year — from 1956 to 2018 — was 2006, when ad sales were about $49 billion.

If you want to know what killed newspaper advertising, look no further than your standard search engine Google and social media site Facebook.

From Yahoo finance, Google had total revenue in 2019 of $162 billion. That's BILLION.

As a media buyer/advertiser, can you imagine how many newspaper ads in the country you could purchase for $162 billion?

Instead of paid print advertising, the new model focuses on search. Search may have single-handedly destroyed newspaper print advertising.

For Facebook, website thestreet.com noted that as of late June 2020, the firm expects "revenue of $78.18 billion and earnings of $7.50 per share for the year, ahead of Wall Street's consensus of $77.03 billion and $7.32 per share, respectively."

Why did search and social media take away the money? Because they claim better return-on-investment measuring sticks for engagement (clicks, follow-throughs and sales). And newspapers believed that: that's the hard part to understand.

Here are some additional facts.

This is from the July 11, 2020 *The Atlantic*:

Here are just some of the dire statistics. Between 2008 and 2017, American newspapers cut 45 percent of their newsrooms staff — and the following years, for many outlets, brought even deeper contractions. From 2004 to 2015, the United States lost more than 1,800 print outlets — some because of corporate mergers and others because of simple closures. Fewer than one in six Americans subscribe to a local newspaper, in either print or digital form. Over the past two decades, the revenue sources that once made newspapers lucrative enterprises — in particular, the money that flowed in from local and classified advertising — has dried up as sites like Craigslist have proliferated and as advertisers have shifted their dollars to digital platforms.

The bottom line is: Google and Facebook are the big winners and newspapers are the big losers for advertising dollars.

The latest on the disaster from the newspaper industry comes in *Bloomberg Businessweek* from July 20, 2020:

U.S. newspapers' cumulative advertising revenue fell from a 2006 peak of $49 billion to an estimated $14 billion in 2018, the lowest in 40 years, according to the Pew Research Center. Google's U.S. ad revenue jumped from $11 billion to $63 billion in the same time frame.

COVID-19 has also wreaked havoc on another staunch content provider for newspapers throughout the country.

According to a story in early August in the *New York Times*:

The history of the newspaper business was on vivid display at a hearing on Tuesday, when a federal *bankruptcy judge confirmed the sale of the McClatchy Company, a newspaper chain run by the same family since 1857, to a New Jersey hedge fund in a deal valued at $312 million.*

The sale of McClatchy, the owner of The Sacramento Bee, The Miami Herald *and more than two dozen other news outlets in 14 states, to Chatham Asset Management was in the works since February, when McClatchy filed for Chapter 11 bankruptcy protection after more than a decade of losses and cutbacks.*

The deal, which will move a prestigious news publisher from family control to an investment company, is in keeping with a broader trend that has alarmed many press advocates, who argue that finance firms are imperfect stewards of an industry built on the watchdog work of chronicling government and commerce.

At the 3 p.m. hearing, Judge Michael E. Wiles approved the result of an auction held last month in which Chatham, a fund that controls more than $4 billion in assets, emerged as the winning bidder.

The hedge fund offered to convert the more than $262 million it owns in McClatchy debt into equity in a Chatham-owned version of the company. It also agreed to throw in roughly $49 million in cash and will pay additional costs, including employee payroll, that McClatchy incurred since filing for bankruptcy.

After the sale becomes official — probably by September — Chatham will become the owner, and the publicly traded McClatchy will go private. The company's chairman, Kevin S. McClatchy, the great-great-grandson of the founder, James McClatchy, and its chief executive, Craig Forman, said they planned to depart once the deal closes.

The company will not be split up after it emerges from bankruptcy, according to the terms of the agreement. In a July 24 news release, McClatchy said Chatham's bid would allow it to retain most of its employees and honor its collective bargaining agreements.

After the judge announced his decision on Tuesday, Mr. Forman said in an interview that the sale would benefit the company he has led since 2017. "Now, with this successfully addressed, McClatchy is very well positioned to go forward and continue to drive what we've built in the last three years, a sustainable digital growth platform for local news," Mr. Forman said.

The runner-up bidder, Alden Global Capital, a New York hedge fund that controls more than 200 news outlets through MediaNews Group, lost out after having offered what amounted to approximately $210 million in debt and cash, according to a court filing. (An unspecified third party made a bid that was deemed insufficient, according to a filing.)

Chatham has a growing presence in the news industry. In 2016, it took a majority stake in Postmedia, one of Canada's largest newspaper companies. Since that deal went through, 1,600 Postmedia employees have been laid off, and more than 30 of its publications have been shut down.

Chatham is also the principal owner of American Media Inc., the parent company of The National Enquirer *and other supermarket tabloids.*

By taking over McClatchy, a consistent winner of prestigious journalism awards, Chatham will acquire 30 news outlets in the United States. In addition to the McClatchy flagship paper, The Bee *— which was founded in the wake of the California gold rush — the chain includes* The Charlotte Observer, The Kansas City Star *and the news agency McClatchyDC.*

The mayors of several cities with McClatchy dailies, including Sacramento and Lexington, Ky., filed letters with the bankruptcy court urging civic-minded local ownership. Sree Sreenivasan, a professor of digital innovation at Stony Brook University's School of Journalism, noted with dismay the absence of bidders who were not part of the finance world.

"It's a sad moment, because that tells you that people who traditionally might have supported local journalism — including people with local connections, local stakeholders — were not there," Mr. Sreenivasan said.

The completion of the sale will extend the finance industry's sway over local news coverage. The nation's largest newspaper chain, Gannett, the publisher of USA Today *and some 250 other dailies, owes significant debt to one private equity fund, Apollo Global Management, and is controlled by another, Fortress Investment Group, which is owned by the Japanese conglomerate SoftBank.*

Alden, in addition to its roughly 200 news outlets, has a 32% stake in another major chain, Tribune Publishing. It also owns a large stake in Lee Enterprises, which publishes The Buffalo News *and roughly 75 other dailies in 26 states.*

McClatchy's troubles can be traced to 2006, when it bought its larger rival, Knight Ridder, for $4.5 billion, plus the assumption of $2 billion in debt. Over the next 12 years, McClatchy cut its work force from more than 15,000 full-time employees to around 3,300, according to public filings.

Chatham started investing in McClatchy in 2009 and became the chain's largest creditor. The fund was the leading candidate to buy McClatchy after the company filed for bankruptcy, citing its inability to meet obligations that were part of a $1.4 billion pension plan.

Chatham is led by Anthony Melchiorre, a Chicago-area native who worked at Goldman Sachs and Morgan Stanley. In 2002, he was let go from Morgan Stanley as part of a round of layoffs. Soon after, he set up his own hedge fund in Chatham, N.J. Some of its clients are listed under a Cayman Islands address, where more favorable tax rates apply.

Hedge funds often find bargains by taking on properties that may seem unattractive. The newspaper industry has been struggling for years as the rise of digital media has cut deeply into advertising and circulation revenue. Roughly a quarter of the newspapers in the United States, most of them weeklies, were shut down between 2004 and

> *2019, and about 50 percent of newspaper jobs were eliminated in that time.*
>
> *Making the outlook grimmer is the economic slowdown imposed by the coronavirus pandemic — meaning the new owner of McClatchy is in for a challenge.*
>
> *"We know the outlook is unpredictable in every single metric," Mr. Sreenivasan said. "How do even the best-intentioned of owners plan for looking ahead?"*

A 2019 PEN America study examines the ultimate conclusions to the decline of print media:

> *The decimation of local news in recent years — specifically the hollowing-out of newspapers and other vital reporting outlets at the city, state, and regional level — represents a crisis for American democracy. When ad revenue dries up, consolidation and cost-cutting gut newsrooms, beats remain uncovered, and corruption goes uninvestigated, the American populace lacks vital information about their lives and their communities. A vibrant, responsive democracy requires enlightened citizens, and without forceful local reporting they are kept in the dark.*
>
> *The consequences of imperiled local news eco-systems for U.S. political and civic life have already been dramatic, and unless we take concerted action, they will only get worse.*

That means areas of readership — regions where the newspaper is sold and subscribers live — will turn into "news deserts." That means the policing that newspapers have been important for — questioning the decisions and behaviors of municipal supervisors and school board officials — will no longer take place. That is scary. There will be less accountability. There will be dirtier deeds kept out of the public purview. It could mean the end of transparency with public officials. Does anybody want this?

Can Newspapers Survive?

When I began in the field in 1982, after growing up with the utmost admiration for the printed word, I never would have thought — the most pessimistic predictions — that newspapers would have crashed and burned as badly as they have.

These days, how can the daily, community newspaper not only survive, but thrive?

They can, however. I will show you how.

First, the book will take you on a journey backward in time, to the heyday of newspapers: the mid-1970s to 2000.

Later chapters examine what is happening today to bring other newspapers to the brink of bankruptcy and failure, including some very close to home.

Those are some lingering questions. Perhaps, based on my four decades in this business, I have some answers.

— Andy Andrews
December 2020

A Reader's Postscript:

Did you know that the original book, CHICKEN SOUP FOR THE SOUL, by Jack Canfield and Mark Victor Hansen, was rejected 144 times by publishers and agents?

This was worse: DEEMED NONESSENTIAL was rejected 161 times by publishers and agents. So we understand adversity but, fortunately, it doesn't stop us from delivering a message critical of what we experience today.

Chapter 1
A NEWSPAPER FAMILY

I remember a soft brown and very comfortable La-Z-Boy recliner, a magazine rack and a reading light.

Of course that was my father's chair.

Andrew Lawrence Andrews, my dad, was a health and fitness teacher at Twin Valley High School in the farmlands of Elverson, Pennsylvania, about 45 minutes west of Philadelphia. His job: instructing sometimes bratty and insouciant middle-school kids not only about muscle groups and nutrition, but also, of course, the birds and the bees.

(Dad thought the best prescription for birth control was to show a film of a live, messy birth to impressionable 14-year-olds. He was raised in the Great Depression. And we were children of parents from the Great Depression, all six of us Andrews kids: so, liked the old saying goes, if we weren't starving, dead or on fire, Mom and Dad didn't really worry about us.)

With my best estimate, Dad was a highly conservative Democrat. The teacher's union was pro-Democrat, so Dad would step in line. But fiscally he was very, very conservative.

"Cut up all your credit cards," Dad would tell us.

Every evening after dinner, I could count on Dad reading the *Lancaster New Era,* from Lancaster County, Pennsylvania, the land of the Amish and Mennonite where I grew up. Dad would read the paper in this order: the front page, the sports section and then the comics.

Today's Chuckle

LANCASTER NEW ERA

Local Weather

How Loved Ones Remember Her

Lindy Sue Biechler: A 'Blossoming' Life Lost

Charged With Embezzling Rebates

Local Insuranceman Accused

Fire Ruins Old Hotel at Marticville

3 Companies

Every evening after dinner, Dad read the afternoon* Lancaster New Era*, from Lancaster County, Pennsylvania, the land of the Amish and Mennonite where I grew up.

I was in awe of the *New Era*. In Lancaster County, the 1970s were the height of an era in which there was a morning (Democratic) paper called the *Intelligencer Journal* and the one Dad subscribed to, the afternoon (Republican) *Lancaster New Era*. Each newspaper had its own staff. Most worked at the same shared desks with different hours.

At that time, newspapers were king. Staffing was robust. Wages were generous. With the proper education and experience, an aspiring print journalist could enjoy a lifelong career in the field.

Every year, in one issue, the newspaper's Sunday edition (the *Lancaster Sunday News*) published a two-page spread (referred to in newspaper lingo as a double truck) with photos and names of employees at the paper for 25 or more years. There were lots of dedicated workers. The owners publicly proclaimed and honored the staff's lifelong service.

It made sense, to me, to join the organization as a career journalist. A fulfilling career. Job security as long as I was devoted to the work.

The newspaper ran multiple pages and sections. For a subscriber, there was a robust paper full of lots of news, features, special columns, comics and advertising. Lots of advertising. It could take quite some time to read the entire paper.

But I recall the advice of Ernest Hemingway to young writers: read everything. And Hemingway meant *everything*.

So I did. I read the *New Era* religiously. Every section.

According to Nielsen, newspaper readers are still educated and affluent, but their ages are more reflective of the general population than they have been in the past. For example, 13% of the U.S. population is 70 or older, and this age group accounts for 15% of the total monthly newspaper audience. The boomer generation makes up the vast majority of newsprint readers. Median age of newspaper print readership is 53.5, according to Nielsen.

A recent Nielsen study found that more than 169 million adults in the U.S. read a newspaper in a month — whether it is in print, on a website or via mobile app. In total, newspapers reach 69% of the U.S. population in a given month.

I attended Garden Spot High School in New Holland, Pennsylvania, beginning in 1972. I remember spending study hall in the library and sitting with a high school classmate of mine, Doug Groff.

Doug reminds me so much of the aging population that remains loyal to newspapers.

I spoke with Doug at our 40th high school reunion in Honey Brook, Pennsylvania, in July 2018. I was ribbing him because I always thought of him as the "newspaperman" and had no trouble calling him that. Like clockwork, at study hall in the school library, Doug would go over to the wooden holding racks that used a "dowel-rod" type of contraption to tie sections of the newspaper together, presumably to keep the entire paper in one piece. A library visitor took the dowel rod to a table, opened up the pages and read.

Doug read the paper with intensity, paging carefully through the newspaper. His attention was rapt, to say the least.

Doug still reads the printed newspaper with his home subscription. Those who love the newspaper want to read it consistently, loyally and abidingly. They are newspaper readers for life.

At the reunion, I let Doug know for all his intensity, when reading his newspaper, that he was an inspiration for my own career in magazine and newspaper journalism.

Every study hall that I shared with him, Doug would read and comment on the news.

A World Before Cellphones

For the millennial and Gen-Y generations, it is hard to imagine the world of the late 1970s. This was a world before cellphones. Video games back then, according to a website called Retrowaste, included Space Invaders, Atari Football, Galaxian, Asteroids, Head On, Star Raiders, Flight Simulator and others.

There was no internet. No text messaging. No Instagram. No TikTok.

News came from, primarily, newspapers, radio and television. That's it!

You didn't have to "download" the news. You didn't have to "print it out," because the newspapers did it all, without wasting your color ink! If you wanted to post a meme, you had a print shop put it on paper and you took out your hammer and nails and attached it to telephone polls or fence posts.

Yes, these sound like primitive times, I know. But because we hadn't seen anything beyond an orange-colored cathode ray tube screen, and a blinking cursor next to numbers and words, and saved everything to a large floppy disk, those who worked news were happy.

Those days make me smile, because the newsroom of the 1970s and 1980s included your snail mail "in" box, usually a plastic or metal tray on your gunmetal, uncomfortable desk; an "outbox" mounted on top or nearby, also plastic or metal; a landline, hardwired telephone with a button you pushed to "dial out"; and a copy tray where you placed your story, typed up on a Remington or Columbia typewriter (I loved the Columbias) with keys that you struck on a ribbon before they hit a rolling platen, on long yellow galley paper. You could use a red pencil or pen to mark it up for a "typesetter." The newspaper employed dozens of typesetters who inputted your copy to a primitive computer that, through various steps, gave you "copy" that could be pasted up (or like some composing room staff at newspapers still used, assembled by hand).

More on that process later, when I get to college.

Back to Garden Spot where I recall Doug and his love of newspapers. I asked him if now, 40 years later, he still reads the daily paper with the same kind of intensity.

"I sure do," he said. "I've always enjoyed reading it."

I've learned some curious things about newspaper readership in my career as reporter, editor and advertising representative. There are two types of newspaper readers:

1. The "news hound." This is a reader who just wants to read news fast, furious and cheaply and is content to receive it on his or her smartphone. They are doggedly satisfied with e-editions and push notifications and really want to spend very little money on subscriptions. The news hound will take e-material any day over print.
2. The lifestyle reader. They want the entire package in their hand, to get the "visceral" feel of the printed, paper newspaper and fold it and hold it open to any

page on a whim. They want to smell the fresh newsprint and ink. They do this sitting at their familiar table in their comfortable chair at their selected time of day with their favorite beverage. News is not just information. It is more than that. It is an entertainment lifestyle.

What do I prefer? I view the newspaper world as a lifelong lifestyle. My priority has been print for at least four decades. But I read the news either in print or smartphone.

I will be honest, however. Most news I read is the print variety and I subscribe to many magazines and journalism journals, including trade journals. It's so much easier on my eyes and mind to read the printed word on good newsprint or magazine stock.

Another Type of Reader

Another type of reader, other than the "newshound" or the "lifestyle reader" is one that bothers me the most. I believe they contribute wholly to the collapse of good journalism.

It's the nonchalant reader. It's a reader who has a very unimposing, devil-may-care view about life. Nothing really matters to him or her. While they are aware of factors and forces that directly impact their life, mostly their work, they will respond only to those factors that directly influence their paycheck. Listening to or reading about the news offers them only one thing: entertainment. And that's all.

I remember listening to a definition of a "typical" newspaper reader in a work of fiction I read right when I graduated from college. They were describing what to them was an ordinary newspaper reader. I don't recall the words exactly, but they went something like this:

"Here is the newspaper reader who just needs something to distract his mind while he rides the subway and train back home from a meaningless job in the city, such as New York. He really cares very little for a lot of things and devotes his entire energy to his job and family. Nothing strikes him very much. If he loses a job and finds himself on the unemployment line, or finds out a loved one is lost to accident or illness, then that affects him. But a war in Syria or Iran? The Middle East is so far away, why should he care? He thinks: Who really cares, anyway? It's senseless, to him, to worry about the things that happen in the news in the world, especially if they don't affect him. He just needs something to keep him distracted on the long ride home."

There is not much you can do about these readers. They would be perfectly content with a lot of social media.

Obsession with Facebook

I have read many interesting articles over the years about America's obsession with Facebook and other social media. One that stood out was a column about how, since the public generates all the content for these sites, Facebook, Twitter and LinkedIn should PAY for it. We should all receive cash for our posts on Facebook, which simply generates more users and allows Facebook and other sites to more effectively market the product.

I agree. We should get paid for our posts that generate click-throughs and potential purchases. After all, other news organizations pay their editors, writers and freelance contributors for the content at the news organizations. Why shouldn't Facebook, Twitter and LinkedIn?

But if all we have, in the end — if newspapers don't survive this COVID-19 recession — are social media, and all we have are unreliable reports, backyard journalists and attic bloggers, say goodbye to consistent, reliable journalism. All we will have, in the end, is infotainment.

Devastating

There's the popular song earlier this century, "When It's Over" by Sugar Ray, about a time when "all the things that we used to know have gone out the window." The COVID-19 stay-at-home, governor-mandated lockdown beginning in March 2020 has been nothing short of completely devastating for daily newspaper ad revenue. Many jobs throughout the print industry have been lost.

I will talk about that in later chapters of this book.

Meanwhile, what was in in the newspaper in the 1970s? At the time, Daniel Cherry was the executive editor (many had the title of editor-in-chief) of the *Lancaster New Era*. I had a chance to interview Cherry when I was in high school. Cherry told me he was promoted from the advertising department to his role as editor-in-chief.

I loved that title, "editor-in-chief," and I hated it when the term was retired in the early 1980s. It conferred responsibility and a take-charge, in-charge attitude to newspaper leaders. It also empowered them to deal with higher management and owners as well as readers. These were the days when the editor-managers had real power over hiring, firing and the "personality" of the newspaper. When you read a paper, it conveyed the hopes and dreams of the editor-in-chief, who set coverage and style mandates and who set the stage for how news would be covered, assigning priorities to the right section editors, who in turn would manage the reporters.

Back then, in the 1970s and 1980s, reporters were assigned "beats." The beat was their area of expertise: there were police beat reporters; court, education, sports, business, obituary, lifestyle, and style and entertainment reporters; and full-time journalists devoted to weather, agriculture and specialty publishing.

Those were the days when some newspaper staff numbered into the hundreds of employees, including some who worked part-time.

Separate staffs were employed for morning editions of newspapers and, in many cases, newspaper publishers would print multiple editions during the day, including late morning and early afternoon newspapers. Afternoon employees, entirely separate newsroom staff, would engage readers in early afternoon and late-night editions.

Remember, back then, there were no online news sources. Nothing was online.

For the *Lancaster New Era*, a typical afternoon daily for its time, there was plenty to read about. Staffing at the time probably numbered about 30-35 reporters and editors. I read the columnists religiously. What was my favorite section in the newspaper? All of them.

All indeed.

The New Era was a Republican newspaper that featured editorials and columns that focused entirely on the Republican party. They would endorse Republican candidates for all offices, city, county, state and federal. They would do that regularly — almost unheard-of these days where most newspapers remain party-neutral. Party-neutral was the stance of the newspaper I would work on very late in my career: the *Reading Eagle*.

More on that later.

But what did I enjoy most about the *Lancaster New Era*? I enjoyed its "look" with easy-to-read type that I use in my writing and emails. I liked the used of photos. I loved the organization of stories. I also liked the conservative approach to stories. There was a great mix of staff-written news and features with wire stories from the Associated Press (AP), United Press International (UPI) and Reuters.

I loved the columnists. I would even read Ann Landers, a staple of the publication.

The comics were lengthy, covering many pages. The printed TV schedule was complete (cable was only just getting underway, so there was room for detail to print on what television had to offer). Sports reporting was robust. Entertainment and other reporting was diverse and full of long-form journalism.

The front page was often crowded with local and national/international news. Where else were people going to learn about what was happening?

Remember, this was an era before 24/7 coverage, before CNN and Fox News. You could wait for 6 p.m. to see Walter

Cronkite or Dan Rather, but why wait to see it on TV when the newspaper arrived at 4 p.m.? And it was the latest news?

This is the way it is, and it was a very different world from the one we are in.

When the newsrooms are reduced, when staffing is eliminated, what happens to news coverage?

Those she interviewed saw local news as more and more shallow and partisan in her book, "Ghosting the News," by *Washington Post* columnist Margaret Sullivan. The collapse of the newsrooms, the firing of staffs, means officials in towns, cities, stations and nationwide suddenly became less accountable.

As a reporter, I thought that, because I was attending municipal meetings, I formed a sort of "police." The media are watchdogs for decision-making at local and national levels. Without the watchdog, who holds officials accountable?

Sullivan, a columnist for the *Washington Post*, is sounding the alarm for community newspapers being bought up and monetized by media conglomerates. Cost-cutting is happening even more so, post-Recession and in the midst of the coronavirus recession. The strain affects how many newspapers can serve in the capacity of public watchdog.

What keeps a community newspaper is having that constant, consistent coverage of government agencies that determine the nature of people's lives. You can't shape a community without providing an outlet for what is happening.

As I wrote this book, looking back into my personal history and experiences with news organizations, I realized the stark changes that have taken place. There was no "working from home." There was no "mobile office." Every writer reported to work for an editor at an office. Period.

It was inconceivable that we could be meeting on a television screen or shipping stories through a thing called the internet. The newspaper office has always been essential as the "hub" of newsgathering.

I can remember accounts from those who were in the newspaper business a lot longer than I was.

When I was working for a community weekly, with ties to a daily newspaper, the social news editor (who edited announcements of weddings, engagements, anniversaries, etc.) used to talk about how news was gathered in the days before Zoom, the internet and email. The primary tool was the phone, a landline that was wired to a headset. With the right technology, you could attach a suction-cup microphone to the handset and record it on tape. You could input your text-only into a video display terminal and save it to a typesetting system.

But that was putting the newspaper together. How was news gathered, other than a phone or by person?

According to the social editor, reporters on shift would often walk down to the local bar. In Ephrata, Pennsylvania, there was an underground bar — literally beneath the main street sidewalk — called the Dugout. Reporters would venture down during their workday to share some drinks, catch up on some gossip and listen to some potential "scoops."

You bought beer in exchange for story ideas. That was a given.

THAT concept — drinking with the regulars to gather news went the way of the manual typewriter in the late 1980s.

Newspapers were so well-staffed that reporters could take time off or vacation and there were enough reporters on hand to cover any beat, any time.

These days, with substantially reduced staffs and consolidation of news coverage, including stories shared across conglomerate-connected sister publications, there is little leeway to ensure beats are covered. Newsrooms are left to scramble to determine how everything is covered. Many times there are no reporters to cover important municipal and school board meetings.

In the recent past, some newspapers have relied on an extensive list of freelancers, or stringers — correspondents — that are paid a fee to report on municipal and governing body events, including school board meetings. But budgets in the age of the coronavirus recession have been drastically reduced and many eliminated. That's what has happened since 2018 and what is left is a "news desert" where meetings once covered for a small fee now don't have coverage at all.

It's a sad state of affairs.

In the distant future, I wonder what the newspaper office will be like?

You won't have to go much further than the year I write this, 2020, to know there will be no "office" for the media conglomerates buying up community newspapers. There will be a central printing operations "hub" that may have some offices for staff. For the most part, reporters will work out of their homes. Stories can be sent via email or other systems. Page proofing can be accomplished via internet links. All news gathering can be remotely done.

What will be lost is the sense of camaraderie, of a news staff working together and sharing ideas freely, of being aware of what others are working on, including a sense of history of what the newspaper has covered. Those creative ideas will be lost in the distances that keep fellow writers apart. And that, ultimately, is sad for the news organization and even more of a loss for the newspaper readership.

In the next 50 years, newspapers will see less major enterprise or investigative stories, decreasing work on series or special reports, a dumbing-down in documenting what is happening with government entities and features that can determine the shape of a community. Readers will get a streamlined package that looks almost the same, day by day, on the front cover: one major question-and-answer or small feature on community impact of an event or organization, one national news piece and a court or crime piece. Inside will be more court and crime reports, as much news wire sensationalism to attract readers as possible and local and national news wire roundups.

There will be a family or living section, of course, with simplistic features on home life and entertainment. There will be a business page. There will be sports.

Sports was once the vanguard of increasing readership for a newspaper. Why? Because student athletes were featured and families could monitor the career of their children in sports by subscribing to the newspaper. This attracted adult and student readership, so it was important.

When I worked as a sales representative, I remember how difficult it was to monetize sports at all. It was difficult to get advertisers, other than golfing clubs. How do you establish a market for sports? Would you try to serve your advertising to parents? Would you try to place education ads in it?

What will the newspaper look like in the next 50 years?

That depends on the size of the market readership.

For markets in the readership of about 50,000 print subscribers, or about 10,000 digital subscribers, I predict the following:

- More emphasis on sensational news, locally and nationally, with more crime reports.
- A need for special sections to attract potential advertisers.
- Delivery will be to a platform that is even more compact than today, with “alerts” every hour.
- Staffs of a handful of news professionals, where once there were dozens of writers.
- E-newsletters will be the established mode of delivery.

But reporting will become even shallower with very little long reporting, or much enterprise or investigative news. Gone will be many special features or series.

The newspaper will print stories about crimes and criminals with one strong national and local story. And some news will become like television: just headlines with brief descriptive copy, and that's it.

In a story in the March 21, 2018 *Washington Post*, "A Once Unimaginable Scenario: No More Newspapers," opinion writers Douglas McClennan and Jack Miles wrote that the very essence of democracy could be threatened:

> *In Britain, too, Prime Minister Theresa May has warned that the closure of newspaper after newspaper is a "danger to democracy;" Britain has nearly 200 fewer regional and local newspapers now than in 2005. The picture is similar in the U.S. A once-unimaginable scenario has lately become grimly conceivable*
>
> *.In the U.S., weekday print circulation has shrunk from a high of nearly 60 million in 1994 to 35 million for combined print and digital circulation today: 24 years of decline. Advertising revenue has cratered, falling from $65 billion in 2000 to less than $19 billion in 2016. Newsroom employment fell nearly 40 percent between 1994 and 2014.*

The writers note that "digital subscription and advertising revenue has not made up for the collapse of print advertising industry-wide. And local newspapers across the country have not been nearly as successful at the digital subscription model as the *Post* and the *Times*."

Will a print edition still exist?

The catastrophe created by the increasing belief that a lot of news is "fake" and the distrust of some reporting organizations may not do local journalism in, but it certainly creates a terrible handicap. Some believe social media will be THE prime news source in 50 years.

According to the March 2018 *Washington Post* column:

> *And then what? Social media platforms make the* sharing *of information ubiquitous and nonstop, but where will that information come from in the first place when all the reporters have been let go? What will happen when the newspaper model — what the government-commissioned report published by Public Policy Forum called "the model of journalistic 'boots on the ground' backed up by a second platoon in the office upholding such hallowed standards as verification and balance" — no longer generates that content at all?*

Will social media have that much of an impact? It already has and continues to grow. Keep in mind how much Facebook and other sites have tried to filter facts from fancy, and how often they don't succeed.

According to a report in December 2018 from the Pew Research Center, social media is outpacing print for the first time:

> *Social media sites have surpassed print newspapers as a news source for Americans: One-in-five U.S. adults say they often get news via social media, slightly higher than the share who often do so from print newspapers (16%) for the first time since Pew Research Center began asking these questions. In 2017, the portion who got news via social media was*

about equal to the portion who got news from print newspapers.

Social media's small edge over print emerged after years of steady declines in newspaper circulation and modest increases in the portion of Americans who use social media, according to a Pew Research Center survey conducted earlier this year.

Overall, television is still the most popular platform for news consumption — even though its use has declined since 2016. News websites are the next most common source, followed by radio, and finally social media sites and print newspapers. And when looking at online news use combined — the percentage of Americans who get news often from either news websites or social media — the web has closed in on television as a source for news (43% of adults get news often from news websites or social media, compared with 49% for television).

Among the three different types of TV news asked about, local TV is the most popular — 37% get news there often, compared with 30% who get cable TV news often and 25% who often watch national evening network news shows.

For the first time, we also asked respondents if they got news from a streaming device on their TV — 9% of U.S. adults said that they do so often. There is a large amount of overlap between those who stream TV news and those who get news on broadcast television — a majority of those who get news from streaming TV often (73%) also say that they get news often on broadcast or cable TV.

Let's take a look at what newspapers once were, and how they operated, before we can determine their future.

Chapter 2

A WRITER'S WAY

Before we step back in time to discuss what newspapers were, no one in the industry from 1975 to 2000 could have predicted the great pandemic of 2020.

Some of us, of course, became "nonessential." I was laid off permanently from my newspaper position as Special Sections Editor in the *Reading Eagle* in April 2020. Was I nonessential? Apparently so.

Reducing newsroom personnel is becoming a dangerous trend.

According to a recent article in *The Guardian*:

> *The news industry, where profits tend to vary between slim and non-existent, has particularly suffered. . . . Scores of newspapers have laid off staff or closed entirely, according to Poynter, and in April (2020), Penny Abernathy, the Knight chair in journalism and digital media economics at the University of North Carolina, told the Guardian she expected "hundreds, not dozens" of newspapers and news websites to close.*

But this acute loss is the result of a long decline, Washington Post columnist Margaret Sullivan writes. More than 2,000 newspapers have closed since 2004: "and many of those that remain are mere shadows of their former selves".

Facebook and Google have borne much of the blame, sucking up the advertising that local newspapers, in particular, once relied on. The 2008 recession meant further losses.

"Round after round of layoffs and buyouts at nearly every paper in the country resulted; local journalists who thought they had a lifetime job covering local government, for example, were out on the street," Sullivan writes.

"Copy editors were deemed nonessential. Unsurprisingly, the quality of many newspapers went down."

The result was many communities no longer having a newspaper dedicated to local coverage, resulting in "news deserts" — areas which have no local news coverage at all. In 2018, a study by Abernathy, at the University of North Carolina, found that 1,300 U.S. communities have completely lost news coverage.

The impact, Sullivan says, is stark.

"Studies have shown us some interesting things. For example, municipal borrowing costs go up when local news declines. Why? Because the watchdog isn't there — and so, local government becomes less

efficient and more prone to corruption or at least wasteful spending," Sullivan said.

ESSENTIAL: Newspapers serve an important role in providing transparency for municipalities, school districts and the residents within. But as staffs decline, local coverage of news has waned, in some cases dangerously. Without the staff, it becomes impossible to cover municipal and school organizational news. What allows the newspapers to survive and retain readership is local coverage.

In Trouble

When COVID-19 reached the pandemic stage in March 2020, I knew we were in trouble.

Newspapers depend heavily on restaurant and retail ads. In Pennsylvania, lockdown — the closing of nonessential businesses — began March 21.

That was a critical blow to a LOT of advertising in local papers. It means restaurants couldn't — or wouldn't — advertise. Most retail locations were shut down. They simply couldn't afford to advertise. The struggle for any businesses to stay afloat had begun.

Also, only essential people — those involved with law enforcement, health care, municipal basic services and similar companies — could report to work or be on the roads. Fortunately, for the most part, working journalists are "essential" personnel.

Still, some were deemed "nonessential." Unfortunately I was one of them.

From the 1970s to 2000s, no one had any doubt that newspaper writers and editors were essential. How else did you get the news? The internet did not become active until the late 1990s, so people's source of news was very, very limited.

At the time I decided to select a newspaper career in the late 1970s, I touted the importance of reporters. We were "essential" in every meaning of the term.

To think I could have chosen a different career path would have appealed to me if 2020 would have happened in, say, 1977.

While becoming a newspaper professional wasn't my immediate choice, in the end, it was favorable compared to another interest of mine: electronics.

These were the days of elective programs in high school. The idea was to allow students to explore career opportunities early and to benefit, long-term, from diversified coursework. I was something of a device geek (my toys were old radios and walkie-talkies), so when faced with having to choose a shop class (what had since morphed into industrial arts instruction), I chose electronic technology.

(That certainly was fitting. For Christmas 1975, Dad purchased the first home version of the video game, Atari's "Pong," for the family. For those who don't remember, Pong was air hockey in electronic format.)

I had an excellent electronics instructor as part of an elective course in shop class: Mr. Fred Erisman. Mr. Erisman didn't hesitate to move me along toward some complex assembly, including a color organ (using field-effect transistors that allowed lamps to react to sound vibrations). I received straight As in electronics.

So Mr. Erisman asked me about what I had chosen as my own career path. I told him I loved electronics, but I also loved to write.

At the time, I was also enrolled in Journalism I with Mr. Frank Palumbo, "Mr. P" as the students affectionately referred to him. Mr. P was adviser to the school newspaper, the *SpartaNews* and the yearbook, the *Spartanus*. (Our school mascot was a Spartan.)

That's when it all changed.

I realized how much I loved to read and write. I never really envisioned myself so narrowly as a "newspaperman." I thought of myself as a writer: I was writing every day in a journal but I was also writing letters to the editor, including tales of growing up in the farmlands of eastern Lancaster County for the *Lancaster Sunday News* (under the guest column "I Know a Story") submitted by readers.

I also read the monthly student newspaper, *SpartaNews,* and contributed letters to the editor.

At the same time I was enrolled in Journalism I, I put together some projects for my coursework. One of those was in October 1977, when I was enrolled in Journalism II, interviewing then-editor of the *Lancaster New Era*, Mr. Dan Cherry.

I remembered visiting the Lancaster Newspapers newsroom, which had desks that were "shared" by both the morning *Intelligencer Journal* and afternoon *New Era*. Back then, newspaper owners celebrated the competition for news from the morning and evening staffs. I can remember some details: papers scattered about with electric and manual typewriters, men reporters in shirt and tie, women writers on the phone, and an "open format" typical of the newsroom with very tiny cubicle-like spaces. And Mr. Dan Cherry, in an office that looked like something out of Clark Kent's Daily Planet, with glass windows and a door.

It was certainly great to meet Mr. Cherry, whom to me seemed somewhat quiet, an executive that seemed to have a subdued workingman's disposition. Needless to say, he wasn't very talkative. What was telling is that I was in awe of him: Mr. Cherry was the editor-in-chief of my family's favorite newspaper. At times, if I recall correctly, Mr. Cherry was mildly cheerful but very composed. He answered questions very simply and seemed patient with a kid such as myself.

(This is coming from the mind of a 16-year-old high school student who was far from mature enough to pick up on many subtleties. I think this is as accurate a memory as I can recall.)

Of course I was nervous. The *Lancaster New Era* newsroom was a strange environment, as different from Garden Spot Junior High School Room 913, the publications room on the northwest corner of the second floor, as you could get.

So I asked Mr. Cherry some questions, including the obvious: When and how did your career begin in newspapers? What do you do as editor in chief? How did you land the job?

I remember his responses. But one thing I thought was telling: he was at one time the advertising director. He was appointed to lead the editorial side. That was strange: a bridge over advertising to editorial. At the time, I thought almost nothing of it. But after my time spent in newspapers, I thought that his "hybrid" attitude was important as a support for both editorial and advertising.

Back then, there was what can only be called the "separation of church and state." Almost like a wall between them, editorial and advertising were supposed to live within their boundaries and not cross over. Advertising was not supposed to influence editorial and vice-versa. That wall was solid and unbreakable. There was no way either side could exert influence and power over each other.

However, it seemed ahead of its time to allow the former advertising director to be editor-in-chief. That "hybrid" position was very unusual for its time.

I view myself as that "hybrid" now, and I have worked on both sides of the fence: editorial for several decades and advertising for about a decade. Of course I wasn't the first to do so.

For the interview with Mr. Cherry, I received an "A" for this project from my high school journalist teacher, Mr. Frank Palumbo. He thought my questions were excellent and the presentation very, very good.

In Journalism II, I was charged with a culminating project. I was able to marry my love for the literature of science fiction with the ability to develop a science-fiction newspaper. (There have been many science-fiction newspapers since, but the one that remains in publication today is LOCUS.) I used the tools I had to come out with a pulp newsprint edition of "Scientifiction," in honor of

Publisher Hugo Gernsback, founder of the pulp magazine *Amazing Stories* that launched in April 1926. In my class project, the print *Scientifiction* newspaper, I published features on my favorite authors: Ray Bradbury and Isaac Asimov, with a report on the 1977 Worldcon, an annual worldwide gathering of science fiction fans. The convention, attended by thousands of fans, presents the Hugo Award for fiction and film in honor of Hugo Gernsback.

I loved to write, and that included letters to the editor. It seemed like a great idea at the time and many things inspired me.

Printed instructions to send in your letters to the editor to the *Lancaster New Era* were always easy to follow.

So I did. About lots of things. I didn't keep copies of them, but I sent them out. In addition, I would help Mr. P type and send out (yes, at this time, via snail mail) news from Garden Spot, including honor roll, honor society and other lists. I would send them to all the newspapers, including the weekly papers and the merchandiser publications. (Back then the weekly town newspaper, the *New Holland Chronicle*, was still being published.)

It was always special when I would see my work in print. That was very exciting!

ESSENTIAL: Since I can remember, I was always strongly opinionated. I was mesmerized by the opinions of the editorial page and entranced by the letters to the editor. That section alone draws millions of loyal newspaper subscribers, even today. Many newspaper subscribers want to feel "connected" to what impacts their lives. That's why editorial

pages and letters to the editor are so essential to the health of the publications.

I thought, why not become more active in the school newspaper, the *SpartaNews*?

So I considered asking to join the newspaper staff, but I was too busy reading a lot. I loved to read above all and I didn't want any work to get in the way of trying to read everything.

(I spent many evenings at the New Holland Public Library trying to devour all they had in the science fiction sections, reading all the Isaac Asimov fiction and nonfiction books the library stocked, not to mention the entire collection of the works of Ray Bradbury. After all, I featured essays about their influence on me as a budding fiction and nonfiction writer for my journalism class project, *Scientifiction*.)

But I couldn't help it. I submitted my first letter to the editor. This one was about the smoking lounge.

Yes, the high-school smoking lounge at the Garden Spot Senior High School.

That was an experiment by high schools in the late 1970s to deal with smoking in the high schools in a very liberal way. Rather than tracking down students Gestapo-like and placing them in suspension after school for lighting up one or two, they allowed, for a brief time, the students to smoke in designated restrooms. Those designated restrooms were in the hallway across from the school library. A frequent visitor to the library, I thought it rude and unhealthy to breathe the waves of smoke anytime we passed the restrooms.

My photo in the high school yearbook, the* Spartanus. *At the time, working toward a career in newspapers seemed the smart thing to do. So I kept reading and writing.

So I wrote about it and my letter to the editor appeared in the November 1977 school newspaper, the *SpartaNews*.

I wonder how much of an impact I had when they closed the smoking lounge barely 2 or 3 months into the start of the concept.

But I was a published writer and proud of it.

I enjoyed working in Garden Spot Junior High School Room 913. It was where my career began. During a recent high-school reunion/walk-through of the school, which I visited with a fellow classmate, we commented to the tour guide about how incredibly small the room was. It could accommodate no more than about a dozen students, tops. And the room was divided into a classroom and a yearbook/newspaper workshop area with one large circular table. One room was a very tiny darkroom, because the 1970s were the days of film process photography, with ammonia baths to accommodate the processing of prints.

Before there were newspaper photos, you had to make "prints" and though the darkroom was small, it was sufficient to process thousands of black and white photos for an entirely black and white 1978 yearbook and newspaper. Newspapers of the time did not feature anything but black and white, cover to cover.

Mr. P took advanced studies at Columbia University in New York to look at new strategies for the high school yearbook staff. He took advanced layout and design courses to create a better yearbook and newspaper for the school.

In the 1970s, remember, there was no internet and social media. When Mr. P taught journalism, it was the newspapers of the time that he taught us to incorporate in the yearbook and school newspaper: expansive features, newsgathering, event reporting, family and home features. It was personality profiles galore. It was reviews of plays, theater, television and film. It was coverage of high school games. Altogether, it was a community organ that worked and was accepted. After all, your first heard about it in the paper, not Facebook!

Today, of course, little has changed. There is one big component, of course, and I think this drains a lot of time and energy from students from putting out a good product: their occupation with text messaging, social media, websites, and all of that has grabbed onto us in ways no one could imagine.

Certainly, in high school in the 1970s, nobody saw the internet coming.

College

I remember walking down the hall to another classroom at the time when Mr. P started walking beside me. He wanted to know what college I was going to select to study journalism. He could tell that's where I was headed. I said it was either going to be University of West Virginia or Temple University in Philadelphia. Mr. P thought highly of both of them, but told me it would be closer and less expensive to enroll at Temple University.

So I did.

But I wasn't finished.

I spent a lot of time listening to the school radio station, KGSH, supervised by Mr. Stan Deen, the brilliant English instructor and radio station adviser. (Mr. Deen was also the founder of Garden Spot Performing Arts). It wasn't long before I was inspired to bring my letter to the editor on the smoking lounge to the radio station. So not long after I spoke to Mr. P, I was on the radio station to read a few of my editorials on a segment called "Viewpoints."

One of them, I recall, was how allocated student lunchtime was far too short. Students needed more time, especially after a sweaty gym class, to shower up, change clothes, walk down the hallway, stand in line for food and eat at a relaxed pace. But inevitably we had to wolf down the food to be able to make it to the next class. Time simply was not on our side.

But at the time, working toward a career in newspapers seemed the smart thing to do. So I kept reading and writing.

ESSENTIAL: One of the many ways today's loyal newspaper subscribers stay connected to trends is through their favorite columnists. It was important for me to learn, early on, how to improve the reader's experience. Today, loyalty to weekly or daily newspaper columns remains very steady and strong. Of course I learned all about "viewpoints" by taking a stand against the smoking lounge. I suppose you have to start somewhere....

Chapter 3
HANDS-ON TRAINING

Remember, newspapers were king. If you wanted to read the latest news, you had three sources to do so: newspapers, radio or television. That's it.

So you could easily have a career in media. There was plenty of money for advertising.

It made perfect sense at the time, for high-school students, to consider a career in media.

At one time late in Journalism II when I was in high school, Mr. P discussed an idea he had for an advanced journalism class.

In Garden Spot High School's 23-year-old history at the time, Mr. P's idea would be something never attempted before. Why not, he decided, start a class called Journalism III and make me a classroom contributor, perhaps editor-in-chief, of the *SpartaNews*?

Not surprisingly, I said, sure, why not?

"Do you want to be editor-in-chief?" I remember Mr. P asking me.

I said, "Will do" or something to that effect.

I can remember sitting in front of the high school principal, Mr. Donald Sheaffer, in his office as Mr. P laid out the parameters of the first-time advanced journalism course. I was sitting there, proud to answer Mr. Sheaffer's questions about what I was prepared to do. It was time to get my career started. It had to start someplace, so why not an advanced high school course?

Journalism III, however, was going to have a rocky start. A very rocky start.

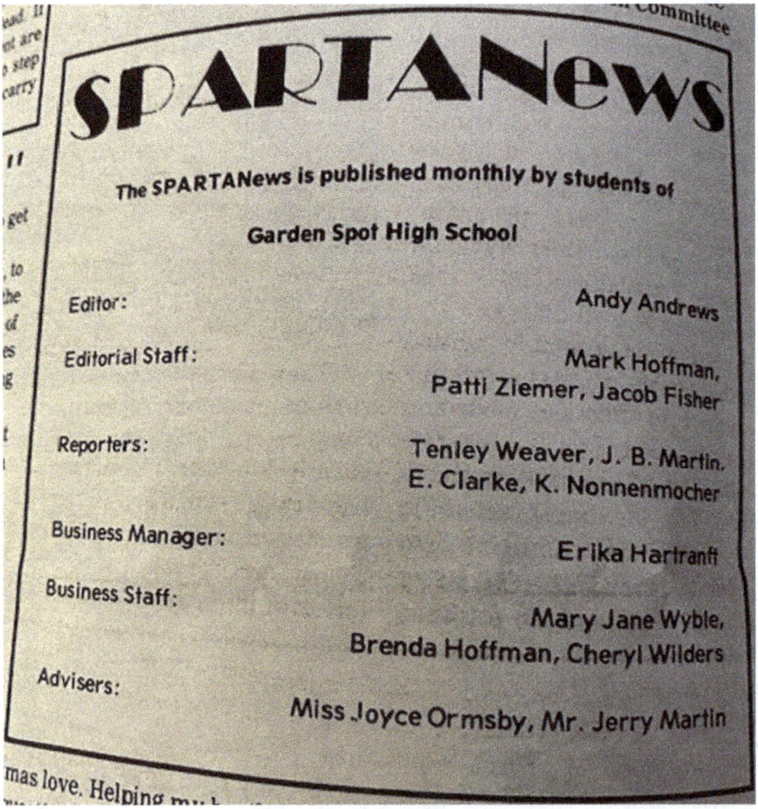
SPARTANews

The SPARTANews is published monthly by students of

Garden Spot High School

Editor: Andy Andrews

Editorial Staff: Mark Hoffman, Patti Ziemer, Jacob Fisher

Reporters: Tenley Weaver, J. B. Martin, E. Clarke, K. Nonnenmocher

Business Manager: Erika Hartranft

Business Staff: Mary Jane Wyble, Brenda Hoffman, Cheryl Wilders

Advisers: Miss Joyce Ormsby, Mr. Jerry Martin

I fondly remember working on the Garden Spot High School monthly newspaper, the* SpartaNews. *Here's the newspaper's masthead.

ESSENTIAL: I am eternally grateful for the open-mindedness of some excellent high school administrators before I began my career. They were extraordinarily supporting and positive and were willing to take chances on students. Thankfully that continues even stronger today, for many schools. And those students are very lucky. Thank you, Mr. P and Mr. Sheaffer!

An Icon Passes

Something felt strangely wrong on a cold Sunday night late in January of 1978. I just finished watching TV and was doing some chores. Something felt wrong, at about 7 p.m., and I couldn't place it. Something felt out of place, but I couldn't figure out why I had a sudden feeling of panic, of formless trepidation. Was it something I ate? Was it something that was worrying me? No. I couldn't think of anything.

I went to school the next day and found out that Mr. P had suddenly passed away, the night before, of a heart attack.

Apparently he had not been sleeping and taking care of himself the past several weeks. He was working very hard to finish the *Spartanus* yearbook deadline and admitted sometimes to us in class that he was becoming frustrated by its progress. Apparently he was pushing himself too hard, because what was a cold soon became pneumonia for Mr. P. He admitted himself to the hospital, where the pneumonia was so severe he died of a heart attack shortly after he was admitted.

The school was in shock. We couldn't believe what we were hearing. Mr. P? Gone? How could that happen?

Because of the news, school officials delayed the start of the second semester until after the funeral. So the delay lasted until Feb. 3, 1978. (That was a strange late start to a typical semester) Apparently, Mr. P finished in time for the deadline. That's when I became eerily familiar with the word "dead" in deadline.

ESSENTIAL: It was at this time I learned that you could literally work yourself to death. The lessons for a work-life balance began for me in 1978 with the death of a beloved journalism instructor.

Be careful. Practice self-care. No print deadline is worth sacrificing your own health and safety for.

But even more sadly, we learned later that Mr. P, who recently married, was expecting his only child, a daughter. In the years since his death, I spoke to his daughter several times about her father. For reasons of privacy, I will let it go at that.

The yearbook staff felt like zombies in the weeks moving forward. Their work at this time would involve finishing up some items, but Mr. P's passionate and emotional involvement in their work had ended. Their inspiration was gone. My mentor had vanished. The few of us who enrolled in Journalism class would be facing substitute teachers until a new adviser was hired at an unknown date.

Before 9/11, before the coronavirus of 2020, before the announcements of the Gulf War, before we encountered any of those horrors in our lives, my Garden Spot classmates had to deal with this terrible loss. We looked at each other with despair, puzzled over what to do next. How were we going to continue without our leader?

Happily, I saved some notes. I purchased a new journalism notebook. I was ready to begin my career. I was already collecting information about college. At this time, I knew my course of action was not electronics at a technical school but journalism at a state university, and I narrowed it down to three: Temple University, University of West Virginia or Penn State.

But first I wondered: what type of high school newspaper will we be producing? What would it look like? Who was going to put it together?

In the beginning, we had the best substitute teacher anybody could have hoped for to take the place, temporarily, of Mr. P. That was Ms. Karen Herceg, wife of science instructor Frank Herceg. As teachers, this pair was fantastic and the students loved them.

Ms. Herceg wasted no time. We sat down and discussed stories. For layout, we would have help from the yearbook staff. In addition, we had the excellent and spirited work of substitute teacher Ms. Bernadette (Bernie) Hoober, who seemed even more excited than we were about the prospects for a monthly student-run newspaper, a wonderful person I knew from my family's Catholic church, Our Lady of Lourdes in New Holland. (Later on, Bernie herself would have a long career as an English teacher at Lancaster Catholic High School).

These were exciting times. The newspaper was king, and we were its merry subjects. It didn't take long for us to figure out what to do. Our first issue came out soon after Miss Joyce Ormsby, now Joyce Ormsby Meyer, was hired as teacher and newspaper/yearbook adviser by the school in March 1978.

(Unfortunately, I have lost that first edition of what the 1978 semester's newspaper looked like, but I remember we had news about the local Future Business Leaders of America chapter, the honor roll and I think an interview with Miss Ormsby.)

Our editorial staff, led by Miss Ormsby, staff adviser and our journalism instructor, with yours truly as editor, included Mark Hoffman, Patti Ziemer (photographer) and Jacob Fisher. Reporters were Tenley Weaver, J.B. Martin, Eileen Clarke, Don Harrold and *Spartanus* Yearbook Editor Kerry Nonnenmocher. We had a great sales and distribution staff in the business office (we paid for the cost of printing with ad sales) lead by Mr. Jerry Martin. I can remember fellow senior Erika Hartranft and her involvement in the Future Business Leaders of America lighting the way, along with business staff members Mary Jane Wyble, Brenda Hoffman and Cheryl Wilders. The business adviser said there were ads sold for the rest of the year, for at least four, maybe even five, editions.

We had the staff we needed. We had the income.

Now it was up to us.

We turned out some great editions, including the April 1978 issue, which had Don Harrold's story about "Controversy Mars Senior Class Elections." Miss Ormsby was away that week, moving from Ohio to Pennsylvania. I wanted to make sure we got a paper out before the end of April.

There was that issue about a controversy, however. So when I was called into the principal's office, I was warned to be sure the adviser, Miss Ormsby, would OK the newspaper before printing next time.

OK! But I did advise the principal that, after all, we had deadlines to meet. I could have been held in detention as a smart-ass, I suppose.

In early April, with my parents, I visited what would become my alma mater: Temple University. It was large, multinational, hip, diverse and exciting: a far cry from rural, somnambulist and sleepy old New Holland. That frightened me at first. The university was completely different from anything that came before. And perhaps since.

And it was a lot less expensive than Penn State, which at the time was in the early stages of a journalism program, or the out-of-state University of West Virginia. I was going to Temple to study journalism at the School of Communications and Theater (now Klein College of Media and Communication). My sequence would be print journalism under the magazine sequence.

I thought I was in heaven. I could see a future.

ESSENTIAL: Keep in mind that in the late 1970s, before the internet, before cellphones, media was available to the public on only three platforms: print, radio and television. Temple University excelled at instructing would-be professionals in all three.

At the time, there were two newspaper families in Philadelphia: The morning *Philadelphia Inquirer* and *Daily News* and the afternoon *Philadelphia Bulletin*. Even radio depended on reading headlines and stories from the newspapers. Newspapers were the vanguard. The pay was excellent and the job security strong.

Journalism students thought that would last forever. We hoped it would. We thought it could. We had no reason to suspect any kind of disruption.

We were so wrong!

For the rest of the year, the Garden Spot *SpartaNews* turned out issues in May and June as well.

In addition to the senior class elections story, April's featured a preview of the May Students in Education for the Advancement of Knowledge, or SEAK program; a "man-in-the-street" compilation of opinions about SEAK; a preview of the Garden Spot Performing Arts play "Cheaper by the Dozen"; a student spotlight on student Duc Tran, a senior who moved from Vietnam to the U.S. in 1975; and sports coverage of the opening season for baseball, track, softball and others.

May issue previewed the new cable TV show "Live on Five," the new *Spartanus* yearbook staff, a preview of the prom, a "man-on-the-street" feature about the cafeteria food and a student spotlight on student Sally Martin. Also included were sports stories on the potential championship of the baseball and tennis teams.

The semester (and my high school) finale, the June issue, expanded coverage over six pages (the equivalent space to today's section A newspapers), on the costs of going to colleges; a feature on Dr. Thomas Winters, head of industrial arts; students selected for a chemistry program; a collage of the year in school and sports as well as from the SEAK week; a man-in-the-street compilation of seniors and their wishes for the coming graduation; a page of poetry; profiles on two graduating seniors; and features about the record-setting track, football, volleyball and other teams.

What fun!

It also featured my story, "Editor Records Year," looking back over the entire year with the things I got myself into (repainting the senior stand at the New Holland Fair, attending the plays "Ramshackle Inn" and "Cheaper By the Dozen" and helping with candy sales for the senior class). I read a Viewpoints segment on KGSH on Dec. 16, 1977, "Indebted to KGSH."

It had my views of the prom on May 20.

It had well wishes for graduating seniors and those we were leaving behind.

Decisions Today

I have a terrible dilemma. The other day a colleague and friend called me about a niece who wants to know about writing. She is thinking of pursuing a writing degree. She wanted my advice.

I am also a mentor to a student who wants to be a writer, attending Alvernia University in Reading. What do I tell her?

In the case of my colleague and her niece, I wanted to be sincere but positive. I asked her if she was certain the niece wanted to pursue journalism Really? My colleague wanted me to keep the conversation positive, but in light of the catastrophe called newspapers, how was I going to do that?

Should I really advise about someone pursuing a degree in journalism?

Here are some thoughts:

- Fact No. 1: It can be a very rewarding career. It does not pay much. If you want to make a lot of money, pursue an alternative course. Newspapers don't make journalists rich.
- Fact No. 2: There is absolutely no job security. Period. Organizations in Pennsylvania, by state law, can hire and fire at will. They don't need a reason to fire you. They can fire on a whim, which I vehemently disagree with. But that's the unfortunate extent of the law.
- Fact No. 3: You can be exposing yourself not only to mental, but physical harm, perhaps even death. According to a recent article in *Forbes*, journalists covering the Black Lives Matter protests are getting targeted:

Forbes contributor Sergei Klebnikov wrote:

As a massive wave of protests unfolded in cities across the country after the death of George Floyd, journalists on the front lines have in many cases been targeted by police, with over 300 so far wrongfully arrested or assaulted, according to press freedom advocates.

The battle continues to cover despite the journalists in harm's way. According to Klebnikov:

There have been more than 328 "press freedom violations" between May 26 and June 6, according to the latest count from the U.S. Press Freedom Tracker, a collaboration of advocacy groups such as the Committee to Protect Journalists and the Freedom of the Press Foundation.

Those numbers are unprecedented: In just over a week there have been more violations than the 150 recorded for all of 2019.

Journalists continue to lament the death of old-style, reliable journalism. It seems that is a popular item these days.

On the website Mumbrella, journalist Kelly Baker, from an article in October 2019, writes:

I started out as a 19-year-old copy kid at a rough and tumble regional newspaper where big stories, written by big men, broke often.

Fast forward 30 years and here I am. Still a journalist, but with no real place to ply my wares.

Journalism no longer exists in this country. Not like it used to.

Newspapers are slowly (rapidly in some cases) dying out and being replaced by online news outlets. But the quality just isn't there anymore. Or, at the very least, it's hard to find.

And yet the first thing I do each day is reach for my phone and check Apple News. I want to know what's going on in the world, even if it is poorly-structured and littered with typos and, occasionally, not even based on facts at all.

Sure, I'm subscribed to more serious and legitimate news sources. But even they're not what they ought to be.

I was mortified to post on the Guardian's Instagram feed that they needed to check their spelling. I wasn't trying to be an asshole, but it breaks my heart to see a prestigious product pumping out statements that aren't spelt correctly.

Don't get me wrong, I have worked online. And I know the pressure to get stories published, fast. And there's nobody to check them and human beings aren't machines — we'll occasionally hit the wrong keys. But still. The craft of journalism itself seems to be dying out too.

Very little of what appears online is written by trained journalists. Very little is researched. There are few interviews.

In an editorial that appeared in late October 2020 in the Daily Local of West Chester, Pa., Lowman S. Henry, chairman and CEO of the Lincoln Institute and host of the weekly American Radio Journal and Lincoln Radio Journal, wrote: "With the current 24-hour news cycle, and cable news networks battling for viewers, reporting has become hyper-partisan in an attempt to find a niche audience large enough to make their programs economically viable."

The burden, Henry noted, is on the consumer to understand the bias of the "news" they are getting and to dig deeper to learn actual facts.

"It is necessary to do this because this is the year journalism died," Henry wrote.

In 1980, when I entered the field, there were plenty of morning and afternoon newspapers published in medium-sized cities. The small-town weeklies were still being published. The field was healthy, growing and robust.

Next up: Temple University, the demise of the *Philadelphia Bulletin* and my two-year stint as reporter at the daily *Temple News.*

Chapter 4
CITY PAPERS

It was time to make a decision about which college to enroll in.

Beforehand, I narrowed the choice of colleges down to two: University of West Virginia in Morgantown, W.Va. or Temple University in north Philadelphia.

(At the time, Penn State University appealed to me; however, they had an undeveloped school of communication. And the cost was just a little more than Temple.)

Immediately, when I saw the out-of-state costs at the University of West Virginia, I was stymied. It was going to be far too expensive and too far from home.

I found out a lot of about the dynamics of college costs by working on a feature that I bylined for the June 1978 edition of *SpartaNews*, "Education Proves Beneficial." When I dug up that old newspaper, in very good condition because of the heavyweight paper stock it was printed on, I came across this paragraph:

> *The state colleges are the least expensive. Generally, it is less expensive to attend Millersville, West Chester, or Elizabethtown than Penn State or*

Temple University. Price ranges for state colleges are from $2,000 to $5,000 ***per year***.

(PER YEAR! Emphasis added.)

Kutztown ranks as the least expensive, where prices range somewhere around $2,100.

Per year!

I'll give you a matter of perspective of how ridiculous college costs have become since 1978.

ESSENTIAL: When I enrolled at Temple University, the cost of tuition and room and board for the first semester of 1978 were about $1,200, or about $2,400 per year (with three full meals). The cost has not only skyrocketed, it has gone into the far reaches of space: I did the Temple calculator online (https://bursar.temple.edu/tuition-and-fees/tuition-rates) and, for one year, with full-time college credits, room and board and full meal plan (two meals a day), cost is — ARE YOU READY FOR THIS? — $32,204. That's 13 times more expensive than when I enrolled.

To give you even more perspective, think about this:

My starting salary out of college, with a job as assistant editor at Chilton Company in Radnor, Pennsylvania, was $13,680. If you apply the calculations, I should have been paid 13 times as much, or $177,840, after I was graduated.

And we wonder why student debt is so high, crushing the hopes and dreams of college affordability?

But decision-time came, and I chose Temple University. Besides, my brother lived across the Delaware River in Oakland, N.J. and he could be my transportation back and forth from Temple to Lancaster County, Pennsylvania on the weekends.

Before his passing, Garden Spot's Mr. P liked my selection.

On a windy but bright afternoon in early April, I traveled with Mom and Dad to the Temple University campus, back in the days when Cecil B. Moore Avenue was Columbia Avenue and campus life extended no further north than a Roman Catholic campus church a half a block above Diamond Street. West Philadelphia began from Columbia and 15th to Diamond and 15th. I won't even talk about the east side.

Temple University was like nothing I had ever experienced before: urban, about 30 times larger than my high school (and much, much larger today) with a potpourri of majors and ethnicities that I had never experienced before. The melting pot of society began at Temple, I thought. This was going to be fun. This would be my home for about four years.

I had made it my mission, when school began in September 1978, to study voraciously, to marry myself to the Paley Library system and read all I could (even though I became distracted by the David Paskow science fiction collection, easily one of the finest in the country) and learn, learn, learn.

I realized fairly quickly that the first two years of college would involve studying the humanities, learning the history of journalism and becoming more focused on my curriculum: magazine journalism.

What became obvious to me was a lack of bylines during the first two years.

It wasn't until 1980 that I would realize I needed to develop a written portfolio. I needed bylines. Without a bylined portfolio, I had little chance of securing a job.

I was terrified of joining a newspaper. My only experience at this point was working for a small high school newspaper. The *Temple News* was an 11,000-copy DAILY, for god sakes. It had a STAFF. I would be working with student journalists from EVERYWHERE.

What I came to realize, once I joined *Temple News* as a staff writer in January of 1980, was that, indeed, I wasn't the smartest kid. I wasn't even very bright. I had some talents. So many of these "students" were already working in professional jobs (Mike Brehm, who is at *USA Today*, was a copyreader at the *Wilmington News Journal* as a Temple student.) Some had worked at the *Temple News* for years. I was going to have tough competition.

Fortunately, my news editor, Neil Sheehan, who used to work for Three Mile Island Exelon and is a spokesman for the U.S. Nuclear Regulatory Commission, allowed me to cover a lot of things. Most were things I knew very little, if nothing about.

It was a start.

For the first two years, Temple University was a distraction. Not in the sense that I couldn't concentrate on studies, but that most of my experiences were unique, from discovering how diverse the campus was to all that it offered.

But my ultimate distraction was the huge, 1.1-million book collection called the Paley Library.

I am a big science fiction fan. I grew up on science fiction on TV with "Star Trek," "Voyage to the Bottom of the Sea," "Lost In Space" and many films, including "The Time Machine" and "Forbidden Planet." I read all I could get my hands on in the New Holland Library and the school's annual library paperback book sales: Ray Bradbury, Isaac Asimov, Robert A. Heinlein, Robert Silverberg, Harlan Ellison and many more.

So my focus changed radically and dramatically when I discovered that the Paley Library on Temple's main campus housed the David C. Paskow Collection of Science Fiction in the Contemporary Culture Collection. According to Temple's website, the collection was established in 1972 when Temple University Libraries acquired 5,000 science fiction paperbacks from the personal library of the late David C. Paskow, a Temple alumnus.

Oh man, I was a parched man wandering lost in the desert coming upon a cool and welcoming oasis. I was able to page through the very first issues of printed science fiction, from the April 1926 launch of *Amazing Stories*, edited by Hugo Gernsback to the first issue of *Astounding Stories of Super* Science from January 1930.

Wow!

And first editions from publishers beginning in the 1940s, from Shasta, Fantasy Press, Gnome and many others.

I felt honored to hold some of them in my hands: the foundation of my favorite pastime, reading.

The collection housed a lot of independent magazine publishers as well, with titles I had never heard of before. From the Temple University Libraries webpage, this list includes Liberation News Service, an alternative news agency active in the 1960s and 1970s that documented Third World politics and the American social and political protest movements of the period; the Committee of Small Magazine Editors and Publishers, a small press clearinghouse; G.I. Papers, underground antiwar newspapers produced by and for enlisted members of the U.S. Armed Forces; *Seven Days* and the *Socialist Review*.

In the collection, I was like the toddler discovering a new toy. I spent hours, days and weeks looking through what they had and learned a lot about the world of the alternative press; I read through all issues of LOCUS, the trade publication for science fiction literature, from the beginning; I was like parched field corn with leaves spanning high and wide, sucking in any moisture from the sky.

At Temple University, one such distraction was helping to start — with the assistance of my best friend at Temple, Carl Spicer, a radio-television-film major — a fanzine called OGRE. I was trying to find a speculative fiction/fantasy answer to the slick big-media publication OMNI. Carl and I thought OGRE made sense, so we decided to launch it in 1979 after attending the 1978 Philadelphia Science Fiction Convention at the George Washington Motor Lodge (since torn down to make room for the Route 202 superhighway) in King of Prussia, Pennsylvania.

We didn't think much of or know the guests of this convention at the time.

(Guests were science-fiction writer Joan Vinge and some guy named George R.R. Martin. Martin brought his collection, A SONG FOR LYA, to the convention and spoke about it. The collection is quite good. I reviewed the book in OGRE.)

We published three issues of OGRE at Temple, filled with author interviews, including the last issue that earned me an "A" in magazine production for a culminating project. It was mailed out to a list of friends and I made sure most independent book stores in Philadelphia and the rest of the country received a copy. We interviewed the first editor of OMNI, Ben Bova, at Philcon, which was downtown at the Ben Franklin Hotel, I believe in 1980, and published OGRE 3 in 1981. What a year.

ESSENTIAL: High school and college publishing projects do a LOT to promote professional experience and provide confidence to aspiring student journalists.

Newspaper Changes

What was happening to newspapers in the late 1970s and early 1980s?

A lot. There was exponential growth in the Sunday and other editions with the Philadelphia newspapers, including the morning newspaper, *The Philadelphia Inquirer* along with the blue-collar, subway newspaper (at least that's how some professors referred to it), *The Daily News*. The evening newspaper was the family-owned *Philadelphia Bulletin*, which had a famous slogan: "In Philadelphia, nearly everybody reads The Bulletin."

Not all of those newspapers would last much longer, however.

What happened?

ESSENTIAL: Many of us became inspired to have a newspaper career. We grew up watching Orson Welles in "Citizen Kane." We watched the 1976 film, "All the President's Men," and were enamored about the characters, **Washington Post** ***reporters Bob Woodward and Carl Bernstein, portrayed by Robert Redford and Dustin Hoffman, respectively. Respect for reporters was at an all-time high.***

This was before the internet, before social media, before smartphone technology. In this order, the three main sources of news in the 1970s were newspapers, radio and television.

Newspapers, you see, were king.

Newspapers paid a pretty good salary. After a group of us journalism students toured the *Daily News*, we found out that, with five years' experience in 1980, a reporter would be hired at the *Daily News* at $25,000 a year.

That was excellent money in 1980. According to saving.org, $25,000 in 1980 was equivalent to making about $84,000 today.

Entering a journalism career seemed to make sense at the time.

It sure seemed that way, until the inevitable happened.

The inevitable was consolidation.

No, that's not the right word: more like market grab. It wasn't enough for the Knight-Ridder-owned *Philadelphia Inquirer* to be competitive. They had to destroy the competition from the *Bulletin*.

Want to know what Knight-Ridder did?

It was a shock, a really devilish decision at the time, for 1980 and 1981, and now would be perceived as business as usual: the *Inquirer* dropped its advertising rates severely. The chain-owned morning edition knew the *Bulletin* couldn't do the same. When advertisers departed for the much-less-expensive *Inquirer*, the *Bulletin's* fate was sealed: go out of business, which they did not long afterward, in 1982.

There was only one major daily newspaper in town: the *Inquirer*. (Today, the *Philadelphia Inquirer* is a public benefit corporation owned by the nonprofit Lenfest Institute for Journalism.)

It was a sign of things to come.

But I had my own career as a *Temple News* reporter to work on. I had to build my writer's portfolio.

On St. Patrick's Day 1980, I visited the *Temple News* office to speak to the news editor (I don't recall who it was at the time). I told him I was ready to write. I immediately was assigned to cover a speech by Ze'ev Binyamin Begin, son of Israel's prime minister Menachem Begin, at Temple University's Hillel House. I knew little about what Binyamin was going to say: but he was accommodating and erudite, to say the least, and my first *Temple News* story, "On the crisis," was published in the March 18, 1980 issue.

At the time, *Temple News* was an 11,000-copy free-circulation broadsheet student newspaper distributed for free to honor boxes (the free pickup racks and boxes) on all Temple campuses. I worked throughout 1980 on various assignments, including one that garnered me a Hearst Award nomination (the Pulitzer Prize for college reporters and editors): "CIA Recruiting Temple grads" in the Oct. 7 edition. The story focused on a recruitment push for students in data processing and documented my efforts to find out more about the CIA in Philadelphia. What fun!

In 1981 I was a prolific writer at the *Temple News* with many front-page stories. At the time, Felix Winternitz was editor; news editor was Neil Sheehan, who used to work for Three Mile Island Exelon and is a spokesman for the U.S. Nuclear Regulatory Commission. Neil promoted me to news editor after he became editor of the *Temple News* in January 1982. Unfortunately I had to turn Neil's wonderful offer down because I was graduating from Temple in January 1982.

For my work at the *Temple News*, the story I was most proud of, however, was published on Feb. 3, 1981: "Chapel turns 30; but disrepair greets anniversary." I would like to think my story was somewhat instrumental in the subsequent drive to repair and remodel the Baptist Temple. In early 1981, however, the chapel was dilapidated and condemned, a hulk of what it once represented to the university.

Simply put, the university ran out of money to refurbish it.

For my work at the Temple News, the story I was most proud of was published on Feb. 3, 1981: "Chapel turns 30; but disrepair greets anniversary." I would like to think my story was somewhat instrumental in the subsequent drive to repair and remodel the Baptist Temple. In early 1981, however, the chapel was dilapidated and condemned, a hulk of what it once represented to the university.

But the temple reopened with a lot of fanfare in the spring of 2010, fully refurbished and ready for the public.

Other front-page stories featured a Temple professor who was instrumental in working on the mirror installation on the space telescope; a story on the work of Temple scientists on an anti-aging steroid hormone, dehydroepiandrosterone, or DHEA; and a human protein at the center of attention in cancer treatment at the time, interferon. (My mother's recent diagnosis and death from ovarian cancer inspired me to write this story.)

I can remember typing first-draft *Temple News* stories on inexpensive, long, galley-style yellow paper using a manual Olympia typewriter. These were the days before pagination and even before laser printing.

In those days, after the galley I had hand-typed was copy read, a typesetter retyped the story into a second-generation phototypesetter, essentially a monitor and keyboard with a floppy disk. In this case, the disk was then inserted into a phototypesetter machine, and out came what the layout professionals referred to "wet copy" which, in galley form, on soft or resin-coated paper, was hung up on clothespins to dry. After drying, the galley was placed through a roller-waxer (using a paraffin wax adhesive). After that, a "paste-up" person took an X-acto knife and cut out the columns of type. The columns were hand-placed on a Chicago BlueLine grid sheet: paper with blue grids placed on a light table and, by eye and hand, the paste-up person aligned the waxed columns on the paper grids. When the waxed type was correctly on the page, it would be hand-rolled.

Those blue-lined pages were sent to be photographed and negatives were developed. The negatives went to a plate-maker in forms that were mounted to a web press, where the newspaper was printed, folded and ready to distribute.

That was how it was done in the late 1970s and early 1980s.

Sometimes I had the chance to use the newspaper's typesetter, a CompuGraphic MDT 350 terminal with a 5 ¼ floppy disk, monitor and keyboard that was linked (hardwired, of course) to a CompuGraphic Trendsetter 88 paper processor. The whole process of re-keyboarding and outputting type took quite a bit of time, not to mention cutting and hand-waxing the paper columns. In the day for newspapers, everything was done by eye and hand.

Today, when you look carefully at old newspapers, you can see crooked headlines and misaligned type. (Hey, paste-up professionals were only human.)

I can remember my work schedule for the *Temple News.*

I believe they opened at 11 a.m. I would attend class, grab a lunch if I could at the dormitory, and head over to the news for assignments between noon and 1 p.m. I would talk to the assignment editor, usually the news editor, about what was available to cover: they would provide a choice of two or less. (This operated as a bona fide news room, remember.)

I would make a few calls and take notes, or visit the department, which was easier if I didn't have an afternoon class. Regardless I would begin working the story when all the notes were in, which was usually around 5 p.m. or so.

Many times I remember skipping supper and staying late, typing up the story, receiving additional input, all the cool things a journalist experiences in a working newsroom. The *Temple News* of 1980 was very robust, with separate offices for the editor-in-chief, a news desk, an enclosed office for the entertainment editor and a sports cubicle. A separate office existed for the business staff, busy selling advertising.

If I had another class, I would go and then immediately return in the late afternoon or early evening. Deadline was 10 p.m.

In my four-decade professional career, I have never missed a deadline. NEVER.

In 1981, working at *Temple News*, I was married to my first wife. She realized how devoted I was to the work. If I can recall correctly, one night I didn't return home until 1 in the morning. I was either a fool or completely self-confident that, walking the streets of North Philly at 1 in the morning, I wasn't mugged or questioned by police.

Lucky me, because I was satisfied by the stories I wrote. Those were the days.

Would I do this again? Oh you bet. It continues to be a fantastic feeling as a journalist to see your work in print. Of course, I would have regrets that, in some ways, I could have been too short-sighted in how something was written. Journalists live with some regrets.

My final story for *Temple News* in early December 1981 was about how the science laboratories were shoddy in securing dangerous chemicals and what steps were being taken to ensure student safety. However, editorial space in the last issue for the semester was at a premium and the story never appeared. (I had to get used to rejection. It wouldn't be the first time.)

In the meantime, I was submitting articles to the *Lancaster Sunday News'* "I Know a Story" feature. One that appeared in the Sept. 20, 1981 issue was on the accidental death by drugs of a childhood friend, a feature called 'The Infant Terrible." The other was on Mr. Frank Palumbo — Mr. P — from high school, "The Lion in the Winter," from the Jan. 24, 1982 *Sunday News*. A third was much later, on Aug. 28, 1988, "Learning to fly with latter-day Wright brothers," about growing up in New Holland with a good friend whose brother and an acquaintance built replica sailing biplanes and actually flew them on a nearby farm field.

But I had a career to make.

Chapter 5
CAREER PATH

I focused on my professional, written portfolio.

As an aside, I did not enter newspaper work right from college, despite my work on the college newspaper. I interviewed and gained a position with a large magazine and book publisher, first. Newspapers would come a little later, fortunately.

I gathered the dozens of Temple News clips and assembled them into a carrier-acetate sheet portfolio, from my work on *SpartaNews* all the way through two years at *Temple News*. I saved everything. I still have the original clips under acetate.

But remember, these were the days where newspapers and newsletters were king. There was no internet. Thus, there were no social media. If a company wanted to communicate, there was the newsletter. It was sent via snail-mail.

ESSENTIAL: In the early 1980s, there were few ways of spreading news: newspaper or newsletters, which were either door-delivered or snail-mailed; radio, which simply read the covers of existing newspapers; or television news. That's it. Newspapers were absolute lord of all they surveyed. The

news that radio offered and even television dovetailed with what the print media did. At the time, staying with a newspaper career would have been the right choice. After all, newsprint was king.

But the daily deadlines and my school studies, in combination, were exhausting and stressful. I thought of the stress of having daily deadlines and I just wasn't in love with working for daily newspapers at the time.

I was adept at monthly deadlines and felt that was a comfortable choice.

I graduated in January 1982 from the School of Communications and Theater (SCAT), now called Klein College, with a bachelor of arts in journalism. I was too busy starting my career to worry about a graduation ceremony; and, after all, I took a job on Jan. 5, 1982 with Alphabet Graphics Inc., a typesetting and preprint service in Centerville, Lancaster County; so I did not attend the graduation ceremonies.

I worked as a typesetter using an AM Varityper system (if my memory is correct). I remember having to take ticker tape from my keyboard/monitor system and input it into a phototypeset processor, which came out on thicker, drier, rosin-coated paper. That was normal procedures then; it seems bizarre and quaint to think of it now.

At the time, I was interviewing for a job in publishing. I simply did not want to work for a daily newspaper. I interviewed at a headhunter in King of Prussia. I told the interviewee that I could see myself as a health care or science writer at a publication. The man's name eludes me at this time, but I recall the headhunter seemed confused about what I was saying. It didn't work out and I received no offers.

However, the Annenberg building, which housed SCAT at the time, worked hard to set me up with a job. This time it was an opening at the Chilton Company in Radnor, Pennsylvania, the wealthiest suburb of Philadelphia. The magazine opening was for an assistant editor position with Chilton's *Electronic Component News*, or ECN.

I interviewed for ECN in late March and began work Easter Monday in 1982: April 12, 1982.

My journalism degree from Temple was in magazine editing and production, so it was a great fit. Besides, I grew weary of daily deadlines while at the college daily newspaper. I wanted to write the best features I could, but often, looking over my daily newspaper contributions, I would fall short of story intent and structure. I was nominated a few times for the Hearst Award for my college writing, but I felt more adequate working on better-developed stories if I just had more time.

Besides, turning out stories to the tune of 1,000 to 2,000 words a day, or more, seemed a bit much.

My advice to aspiring authors in high school: choose a major that can suit your working style and capacity. If you don't thrill over daily deadlines — if deadlines are your struggle especially with class projects — do not, repeat, DO NOT choose newspapers as a career.

First Job

First up was the beginning of my professional career with an electronics engineering monthly trade magazine.

ECN was direct-mailed to about 95,000 electronic engineers throughout the country. When I interviewed for the position, I spoke to the editor-in-chief, Mr. Hy Natkin: a very reasonable, nice man whom I learned to appreciate the more I knew him. He was my first boss, and one of the top three bosses in my career.

Hy would often remark: "Andy, remember this: Every once in a while, get off the treadmill and smell the roses."

Hy's wisdom about work and life balance has resonated with me to this day. I appreciated Hy as a manager, a mentor, a confidante, and a friend, and I do miss the time I spent with him at the time I began my 40-year career in publishing.

Unfortunately I wasn't diligent in keeping many copies of ECN, a product trade magazine. One I clung to for 40 years is the November 1982 issue, dedicated to Midcon/82, an electronic engineer convention Nov. 30 through Dec. 1 that year at the Dallas, Texas Convention Center. My feature was titled "More the merrier for software-intensive microprocessor development systems." Back then, "microcomputers" were in fashion, with the launch of the IBM PC. At the time, 16-kilobyte systems were the norm. Some really radical designs could handle 1 megabyte. Hard drives were being invented in the form of the 3 ½-inch floppy drives. But most storage was on standard format 5 ¼-inch drives.

Those were the days.

ESSENTIAL: Chilton Company lived and died on what they came to depend on each issue of every magazine: the reader service card. The Chilton magazines assigned numbers to each ad. Those numbers were printed on a self-addressed post card that could be mailed by subscribers, first-class, back to Chilton. If readers wanted more information from an advertiser, they would simply circle the number. Those cards were then sent to the advertiser. It was an almost-perfect return on investment. And just think: the next time an ad representative would call on the advertiser, the rep would offer proof of how many readers were interested in the product.

Here's another interesting observation from my memory of Hy:

Hy always referred to ECN as a tabloid publication. That meant of course the full-color, slick publication was half the size of a typical "broadsheet" newspaper.

Newspapers were printed very large and wide back then. That's where the term "broadsheet" comes from.

Most of today's newspapers are the size of ECN's tabloid size, back then.

It just goes to show you how much the newspaper industry has lost. Even the physical size of a typical newspaper has shrunken considerably.

For about a year and a half, I worked on various special issues of ECN. (At that time the publications were "themed" issues.)

Chilton Company lived and died on what they came to depend on each issue of every magazine: the reader service card. The Chilton magazine staff assigned numbers to each ad. Those numbers were printed on a self-addressed post card that could be mailed by subscribers, first-class, back to Chilton. If readers wanted more information from an advertiser, they would simply circle the number. Those cards were then sent to the advertiser. It was an almost-perfect return on investment.

At the time, I came up with an idea for a personal computer magazine. I wanted to separate myself from ECN and work on another publication, so I applied for and received transfer approval to a magazine called *Automotive Industries*, or AI. This was the beginning, after all, of the age of electronic control module computer systems, or ECMs, in cars. AI Editor Ira Black welcomed me to write about computer technology in cars, and I did several articles on the subject beginning in the summer of 1983.

The January 1984 edition of AI featured my story, "Year of the C.A.D." It focused on computer-aided design systems being used by automakers. (There is an interesting photo of an engineer working on what looks exactly like our 1999 Plymouth minivan.)

The March 1984 issue of AI featured "Electronic Control Modules. . . Down with EMR!" about the effects of electromagnetic radiation on ECMs.

The April 1984 issue featured what would be my last contribution to Chilton's publications: "A new shift in on-board computers," about how electronics were impacting transmission systems in cars.

Because I had other projects that demanded more of my attention, I worked with Ira, another good boss, until April, until I was on my way to other, bigger projects.

One of those is the first-ever internet magazine in the time before the internet.

ESSENTIAL: Predating the hedge-fund investor newspapers of today, I remember hearing, in 1982 and 1983, how Chilton Company, at that time part of ABC Publishing, was just a tax write-off for ABC. So this hedge fund idea, of leveraging assets in print and publishing, goes back to the late 1970s and early 1980s. It is nothing new.

Chapter 6
REINVENTION, OUT ON MY OWN

Terry Persun, at the time a writer for Chilton's *I&CS* (industrial and process control magazine), and I published *Philadelphia Computer*, the Delaware Valley computing magazine. The first issue was distributed in March-April of 1984. For $2 a copy or $12 per year for the bimonthly magazine, you could read about new spell-check software; the IBM XT, which cost $3,000; access to newspaper articles throughout the country with Vu/Text, a Knight-Ridder company; the DEC Rainbow 100 Digital Company computer available at Levitz Computer Lifestyles store in King of Prussia and at Entre Computer Center, with three locations; a rundown of photos and reports from several "ham and chip festivals"; the Sperry PC; the Epson personal computer; MicroAge Computer Store; Computer Professionals, an authorized Apple computer dealer with its four stores; the Philadelphia Area Computer Society and its work with local user's groups; Doc's Computer Center in Ardmore, Pennsylvania; the ABCs of personal computers and word processors; Programs Unlimited Computer Centers in Jenkintown; a list of new portable computers; The Program Store; and a rundown of the latest computers from Franklin and Commodore; a used-computer classifieds section; Control

Data StorageMaster floppy disks; and even another Apple dealer, Today's Computers at Strawbridge & Clothier.

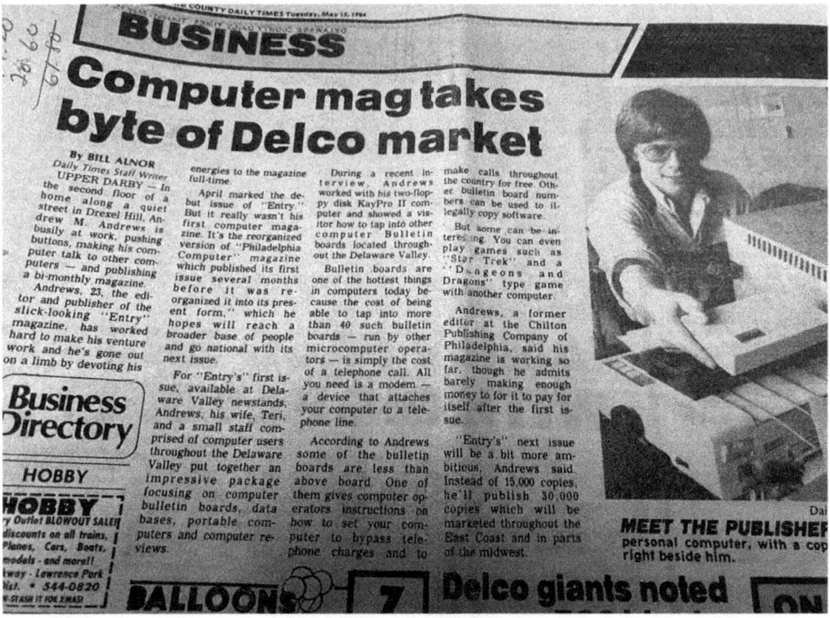

BUSINESS

Computer mag takes byte of Delco market

By BILL ALNOR
Daily Times Staff Writer

UPPER DARBY — In the second floor of a home along a quiet street in Drexel Hill, Andrew M. Andrews is busily at work, pushing buttons, making his computer talk to other computers — and publishing a bi-monthly magazine.

Andrews, 23, the editor and publisher of the slick-looking "Entry" magazine, has worked hard to make his venture work and he's gone out on a limb by devoting his energies to the magazine full-time.

April marked the debut issue of "Entry." But it really wasn't his first computer magazine. It's the reorganized version of "Philadelphia Computer" magazine which published its first issue several months before it was reorganized it into its present form," which he hopes will reach a broader base of people and go national with its next issue.

For "Entry's" first issue, available at Delaware Valley newstands, Andrews, his wife, Teri, and a small staff comprised of computer users throughout the Delaware Valley put together an impressive package focusing on computer bulletin boards, data bases, portable computers and computer reviews.

During a recent interview, Andrews worked with his two-floppy disk KayPro II computer and showed a visitor how to tap into other computer Bulletin boards located throughout the Delaware Valley.

Bulletin boards are one of the hottest things in computers today because the cost of being able to tap into more than 40 such bulletin boards — run by other microcomputer operators — is simply the cost of a telephone call. All you need is a modem — a device that attaches your computer to a telephone line.

According to Andrews some of the bulletin boards are less than above board. One of them gives computer operators instructions on how to set your computer to bypass telephone charges and to make calls throughout the country for free. Other bulletin board numbers can be used to illegally copy software.

But some can be interesting. You can even play games such as "Star Trek" and a "Dungeons and Dragons" type game with another computer.

Andrews, a former editor at the Chilton Publishing Company of Philadelphia, said his magazine is working so far, though he admits barely making enough money to for it to pay for itself after the first issue.

"Entry's" next issue will be a bit more ambitious, Andrews said. Instead of 15,000 copies, he'll publish 30,000 copies which will be marketed throughout the East Coast and in parts of the midwest.

MEET THE PUBLISHER
personal computer, with a cop
right beside him.

Business Directory

HOBBY

BALLOONS

Delco giants noted

Terry Persun, at the time a writer for* Chilton's I&CS *(industrial and process control magazine) and I published* Philadelphia Computer*, the Delaware Valley computing magazine. The first issue was distributed in March-April 1984.

But I had plans to make *Philadelphia Computer* so much bigger.

I remembered reading, one day, an advertisement for a Texas Instruments portable computer. There was a phrase that went something along the lines of "this can be your entry into greater computing power" or something like that.

My eyes fixed on the word "entry." I thought, that would make a great name for a computer telecommunications magazine. So I transformed the name "Philadelphia Computer" into "Entry" with the spring-summer 1984 issue.

The subtitle, "formerly Philadelphia Computer," also read "introducing electronic bulletin board, videotext and telecomputing services, systems and software."

(Does anybody remember the movie "WarGames" from 1983? It was an inspiration for the magazine.)

ESSENTIAL: Entry Magazine, based in Media, Pennsylvania, was a vanguard for the internet. Before there was the internet, there were bulletin board systems, or BBSes, across the U.S. For that issue, we listed the BBSes by state. Every one of them.

Entry featured CompuServe's CB Simulator, and features included a rundown of portable computers, the new Tandy 2000, Vu/Text and the NewsNet specialized business database service. There were ads from Dow Jones News/Retrieval and 21st century email from MCTel. And already there were reports of cybercrime, including a computer whiz kid who broke into California hospital records. Cybersecurity was a controversy even then.

Unfortunately I made a bad business decision to use the format of a glossy, four-color magazine, as printing costs continued to skyrocket. There were no "websites" to provide news as an alternative to print in 1984.

At this time, newspapers were print-only, relying on the strength of their full- and part-time contributors to provide lengthy, in-depth, local news and features for a very loyal subscriber base.

But there are similarities between newspapers and magazines that are striking. Both live and die on subscribers who are looking for compelling, unique content. With magazines, the formula remains: provide one-of-a-kind, arresting, strong cover features with items that can be read no where else. Even more so, magazines — to stay viable — cannot rely on canned content provided by feature providers. They must develop their own, proprietary content and stay abreast and ahead of developments, whether they are entertainment sources or trade publications.

Trade magazines are voices for organizations in the trade. Entertainment magazines need the "scoops" on the development of personalities and organizations they feature.

What makes a great magazine is its editor.

That's the message provided by Ex-British *Vogue* Editor Alexandra Shulman. In Shulman's 2017 feature in the Business of Fashion, she writes:

> *What really makes a great magazine editor in today's world? Is the panic (and I use this word deliberately) being shown by all media owners resulting in good decisions being made? And what makes a good decision anyway? Everywhere you go, you hear of resources being cut back, of staff being let go and the word Millennials being invoked by faintly wild-eyed fifty somethings as if they were chanting their personal mantra.*
>
> *Magazines are a business. They have made a great deal of money for publishing companies such as Hearst, Condé Nast, IPC, Time Inc. and many others*

across the globe. They have been the bounty in a crystal swag bag with successful titles able to leverage substantial advertising revenue from clients who want their messaging to be part of a book aimed at a specific and receptive demographic. So, a good decision is one that keeps the cash coming.

Print magazines are not only information and entertainment but also image-defining accessories, endowing the buyer with membership of a certain tribe when carried or even placed on a coffee table or kitchen counter. In recent decades, the market has expanded so much that there is now a huge choice, clearly unsustainable (at least with today's business model), in the number of publications you can buy. The enormous number of titles on offer means that there is less loyalty than there once was, but the majority of buyers still gravitate to a title that endorses their idea of themselves. You chose to be seen with Vogue instead of Cosmopolitan, with World of Interiors instead of House Beautiful, with Grazia rather than Hello. Or vice versa. They also add an incalculable kudos to all kinds of businesses. It's fascinating that Airbnb, one of the most successful digital brands, has launched a print magazine with Hearst.

Magazines, due to their carefully edited content, are specific and generally speak to the converted. They create worlds that appeal to their readers and their advertisers and over time, they have gained a trust and authority. How many 14- and 15-year-old girls have told me that they love to tear out the pages of

Vogue and stick them on their bedroom walls? How many walls have been plastered with New Yorker covers, still a celebrated marker of the times? In all the research we did during my recent years at Vogue and in my personal connection with readers at talks and other events, the remaining appeal of the physical object was startling. Every time I questioned a group of students whether they still felt the print form of the magazine was valid, the answer was a resounding yes. Certainly Vogue, due to its position as a treat and a luxury, is in a different position from some other titles. But I remain convinced that the appeal of the tangible experience of a thick glossy magazine remains strong.

Back to my own publication that focused on computer telecommunications, *Entry* magazine.

The final issue of *Entry* came out in November 1984. Ads appeared from NewsNet, CompuServe and modems from MultiTech Systems. This issue looked into the first cybercriminals, what we learned were "Telepirates: Criminals of the Computer Age." One way to thwart unwanted access was the Gateway system from Adalogic. This system required an ID and password.

Also included in that issue of *Entry* were the Delphi information, communications and entertainment system; a feature on the "WarGames" movie and its adverse effects on BBSes; how to start a BBS; exploring public domain software; another list of all known BBS systems in the country; an article on portable computers; fighting software pirates; the Radio Shack TRS systems and BBSes; and a story about a man in California who had his computer system confiscated by the police when they found it contained illegal credit card and Sprint access code postings. Hacking was the name of the game, for some folks, even then.

But I couldn't make the publication succeed. I had poor management skills and instead of adjusting to a lesser (newsprint) format, I decided to close *Entry*. It's too bad, since I had a lot of fun.

ESSENTIAL: Did the creation of Entry actually put in motion the causes of the demise of newspapers? In helping to create the internet, did I, unintentionally, help create the demise of the printed newspaper?

After the close of *Entry*, I was involved as a retail representative for Radio Shack Tandy Computer Center (who had a lock on the industry at one time and should be bigger than Apple right now). I also spent some time with a couple of Department of Navy contractors, including SEMCOR and RBC Inc. in Warminster, Pennsylvania. At SEMCOR, I developed the SEMCOR Style Book and wrote and published the guide for the Naval Air Development Center's testing facilities detachment in Key West, Fla.

ESSENTIAL: At the time of my work with defense contractors, with the national budget cutbacks, senior technical editors were deemed "nonessential" employees and RBC Inc. represented my first layoff. I should have seen this coming.

For a time, I worked with Lukens Corporation in Coatesville, Pennsylvania, as communications specialist and editor of *Lukens Magazine*. The Vol. 8, No. 1 issue of the magazine, February 1989, included articles about safety at the steel mill; a story about ENCOAT, a Luken's company, specialists in utility pipe coatings; Simplicity Engineering, a Lukens' subsidiary company's work using computer-aided design and computer-aided manufacturing; the works of the Lukens Foundation; a photo contest with submissions for all Lukens Inc. employees; and a word search.

The last issue of *Lukens Magazine* I worked on, Vol. 8, No. 2, May 1989, examined the work of Lukens Development Corp. at Riveredge Park in New Castle, Del. Other stories examined a possible extension of voluntary restraint arrangements, or VRAs, to keep foreign producers from dumping cheap steel on the U.S.; underground storage tank protection by Cathodic Protection Services in Houston, Texas; lost-foam casting from Simplicity Engineering in Durand, Mich.; National Capital, Bladensburg, Md., a customer for Lukens' Safety Products Group, including Services and Materials, a Lukens company at the time, based in Elwood, Ind.; and a profile of a sales representative who fixed a steam locomotive, engine 1225 of the former Pere Marquette Railroad.

You've no doubt heard that past can be prelude. That is the case with me, since more significant, and long-lasting work, was yet to come.

ESSENTIAL: And more changes were to come. Lukens was purchased by Bethlehem Steel. Prior marketing departments were dissolved, deemed nonessential to the new employers. Layoff No. 2. Here we go again.

Television

I grew up with Walter Cronkite, with his saying, "and that's the way it is." As a kid, I watched the news with Dan Rather, recalling the reports of the body bags, consistently at the top of the news hour, returning from Vietnam. Sadly, I think the country as a whole, the views of TV news, became desensitized to the losses. These were human souls coming back from a devastating war, soldiers with families that would have to endure a gut-wrenching loss, and in the end, after a time, the reports became background noise, blended sufficiently into the oblivion of teleprompters and voices emanating from a speaker.

Why was TV so important to newspapers at one time? Why was it respected?

TV news casts I think did their best to emulate the best practices and ethical structure of a newsroom. They would gather the facts, verify them and check them again. Importantly, they would share the news and give a plug to a newspaper when necessary. It lent credence and culpability to what the TV journalists were doing, and it made what they did believable.

Since the internet and the drive for viewership, the ethical intents emulated by television news got lost on the way via TV report sensationalism, showmanship and story "angling," laziness and a quest to capture markets. And for one, television gave away news for "free" (as they were mandated by the Federal Communications Commission): this put pressure on newspapers because, in the end, both platforms depended on a shrinking advertising market.

Here's an example of how television news reporting, compared to newspapers, sometimes goes terribly wrong.

When I was business editor at the *Reading Eagle*, I remember one of our reporters what assigned to contact the police department over a report on a local TV station about a "fight at a park." Apparently the TV station ran with a Facebook posts that noted there was a fight, which drew police. So the reporter checked: the broadcast was wrong. There was no fight.

Now if a newspaper had an errant report, they would be obliged, followed by reader complaints via phone, email or letters to the editor, that the newspaper check into it and post a correction. But TV? On TV, news is ephemeral; it disappears as fast as it is created. There is little to no follow-up on stories like this.

Keep in mind that there are some excellent TV news organizations. Not many, however. Many have lived so long on irresponsible reporting that it is hard to justify why they still have viewers. And there is less editorializing than there used to be, especially in the early 2000s, where "spin" and "opinion" were brought to bear with almost every news report. (Anchor: "What do you think of that, Reporter Bob?" Bob: "Oh, I think the township should do the right thing and bring back the guillotine.")

Oh, I remember those days and I shudder about so-called "journalism" on television news. This is mere infotainment: some shows masquerade as legitimate news broadcasts. Sadly, that's why I stayed clear of TV news, because in the years post-Walter Cronkite, I have been too worried about how much television news observes best practices and ethics.

Long ago, I had a chance to be a TV broadcast journalist.

In 1989, I was interviewed by Maryjane Landis of Lancaster, Pennsylvania's WGAL TV 8. Landis hosted a kids' show, "Percy Platypus and His Friends." She was on-air host and co-creator of the Saturday morning children's program until 1974. Landis then created and produced "Sunshine Corners" from 1974-1979. Landis passed away in December of 2015.

Landis wanted me to accept work as the morning anchor, a job held at one time by Brad Hicks, who was hired instead as morning anchor and then moved up to nightly anchor at the station. Hicks subsequently worked for Milwaukee's WITI Channel 6 for some time. After Hicks, the WGAL job fell to, I believe, Jere Gish, who is there today.

I spoke to Gish recently about the challenges of reporting and staying viable under today's realities. TV news is also facing revenue challenges that mirror print journalism. But during COVID-19 and subsequent lockdowns, with more people quarantined at home, TV viewership remains strong.

Why didn't I get the TV job? I had no video editing experience. Landis suggested I would do so because I was an established writer and the graduate of a great school, Temple. Landis liked my voice, I suppose. (Many people suggested I have a "radio voice," whatever that means.) But with no video editing experience, a job like this wasn't within reach.

Chapter 7
WEEKLIES
LOCAL AND ONLY LOCAL

As it was in 1990, so it was in the early 2020s.

ESSENTIAL: The weekly newspaper has always been significant because of its focus on the community. The readership is extremely loyal. Homeowners, business entrepreneurs and permanent residents of a community want to know what is going on in their townships, school boards, schools, local organizations and church groups. The need never waivers. If anything, these days especially, local news reigns supreme and is the primary reason people subscribe to a newspaper.

But in the early 1990s, as international news became prevalent on online systems such as CompuServe, America Online and others, readers became more obsessed with what was going on in their community. Who published the news? Weekly newspapers, of course.

One such weekly was a trade newspaper for the agricultural industry — the farmers and processors — in the Northeast. It is called *Lancaster Farming*, published each Saturday and headquartered in Ephrata, Pa.

Lancaster Farming *newspaper, from the start, understood the importance of proprietary, local coverage from its beginning in November 1955 until I helped celebrate its 50th anniversary in 2005. Here's a front-page photo I took for a September 2005 issue.*

At Lancaster Farming, I was hired in January 1990 to replace a woman named Lisa Risser, a livestock reporter for *Lancaster Farming*, who was leaving the newspaper. For a short time, Lisa introduced me to the farming industry that I knew little about in Lancaster and surrounding counties in Pennsylvania.

Readership was very strong and loyal. Circulation was at 45,000 and growing, direct-mailed to farms and agribusinesses throughout the eastern states.

With its trademarked mailbox markets, the newspaper captured the business of a very complex field. Farmers grew dependent on its news, but especially for the ability to use the department to buy and sell commodities and equipment.

To this day, the newspaper's mailbox markets allows *Lancaster Farming* to thrive.

Importantly, as a weekly, it served a common need: stories that you could not find anywhere else, about producer groups, organizations that looked after the farmer/producer, young farmers learning the ropes, rural organizations critical to farm prosperity and the 4-H and FFA youth organizations that were to be readers and subscribers decades hence.

It signaled a shift in readers likes and dislikes. Branded along with other weeklies for towns such as Lititz and Ephrata, readers would be loyal if it was the only source for local news.

And that formula worked for decades.

ESSENTIAL: It took so long for daily newspapers to realize how important local content would be to survive. Some newspaper publishers and editors still don't understand how critical local content is, and publish far too much wire story and filler national material. These days, the wire stories and filler material can be obtained from push notifications and news eblasts from media outlets.

What those same outlets can't provide is news about school board rulings and changes, municipal news, local features of award-winning businesses and families and how they contribute to employment and standard of living in the community, along with society news in the forms of engagements, anniversaries and births and deaths.

That's why readership to those weekly newspapers — in this case, the *Lititz Record Express, Ephrata Review* and many others throughout the country — continues strongly.

Why can't the daily newspapers learn and understand this model?

Some have.

Lancaster Farming, from the start, understood the importance of proprietary, local coverage. From its beginning in November 1955 until I helped celebrate its 50th anniversary in 2005, the focus has been on the importance of youth (4-H and FFA) activities and announcements; group activities, especially with local granges and other organizations; producer cooperatives; the major agricultural fairs and exhibits, including fairs in the 67 counties, covering the competitive events and listings/photos of award-winners; and state events such as the Pennsylvania Farm Show in January and Penn State's Ag Progress Days in August every year.

My career with *Lancaster Farming* began auspiciously, in a way: in this case, with the Lancaster County Tobacco Growing Contest, a preliminary to the Pennsylvania Farm Show.

My Love Affair with Agriculture

Why did I take the job as livestock reporter for *Lancaster Farming*?

What I learned in college and in real life is that agricultural remains the exception from the standard economy. While the general economy can be going through the ups and downs of expansion and recession, the agriculture industry is fairly steady.

I always felt connected to the earth and have been a gardener all my life, growing vegetables since I was about 10 years old. I have been growing tomatoes for 50 years at this point.

I also was enthralled with the staying power of a rich, financially sound and rewarding (emotionally and intellectually) field. Agriculture seems immune to the adverse effects of a failing economy. I had seen several recessions since growing up working on a farm in my hometown in New Holland, Pennsylvania. Through all of them, the farmer I knew weathered them well, almost too well.

So I was convinced that a job in agriculture can be prolonged, safe and rewarding.

I was proven correct, as my position with *Lancaster Farming* newspaper has been my career-longest position at 16-and-a-half years.

What was so astonishing — what I learned early at the weekly farm newspaper — is how cooperative farm organizations and businesses are with each other. While some industries are highly competitive (such as the auto or electronics industry), agriculture will let down its guard to help growers and livestock producers to thrive. It has a selfless, cooperative attitude that is unique. In my experience, no other industry works like this (at least not to the extent of agriculture).

The individuals are a joy to work with. There is a sense and sensibility to farm production, a connection to the earth, a feeling of brotherhood and solidarity that I find missing in other industries. Other industries are fiercely competitive. I can understand why.

But the assistance and infrastructure, including university agricultural extension services, in the agricultural industry is astonishing. There is no comparison.

Needless to say it was a joy to work with the communication services of university extension, state and national organizations and companies that served the farming community.

I knew the agricultural industry was exempt from the normal highs and lows of the economy. We were in a long recovery, but with my layoffs because of national budgetary cutbacks (the Gramm-Rudman-Hollings Balanced Budget Act legislation to cut defense spending at the end of the 1980s), I was spooked by instability. Lukens Inc. was beginning to cut production and I lost that job. I escaped three layoffs in the course of a little more than a year as a result of Gramm-Rudman-Hollings, and I was spooked. I needed firm ground to continue my career. I wanted some sense of job security.

So I turned to what I knew was growing and always appeared exempt from the instability of the national economy: agriculture.

I was happy to try something new as well, even though I had a job offer from a publishing company as a page designer at the same time. I tried to start a bidding war between *Lancaster Farming* and a graphic designer position for a company called Technomic: but the editor and my future boss at *Lancaster Farming*, Everett Newswanger, informed me they were not going to be part of a bidding war and I would have to settle for the offer.

Which I did.

My first assignment: The Lancaster County Tobacco Show at the Farm and Home Center in Lancaster.

Mr. Bob Anderson, agronomy specialist with the Penn State Lancaster Extension Office, was my contact for this story. Bob was exceedingly helpful. Back then, as today, Penn State welcomed the press with open arms. A mandate from the college to Extension service offices was to publicize and promote its programs and events.

The tobacco show was a prelude to the Pennsylvania Farm Show conducted in early January each year at the Farm Show Complex in Harrisburg.

My story was on Page 1 with the Jan. 6 issue of *Lancaster Farming*. What an auspicious beginning to what would amount to a 16-and-a-half year career with the farm publication, mailed at the time to 45,000 subscribers throughout the East Coast. Today, circulation is approaching 60,000 and the editorial staff has more than doubled in size.

Dauntless, I learned about the agriculture industry in the Northeast extraordinarily fast. My second assignment in January 1990 was the Pennsylvania Farm Show. I went to cover the livestock judging events on the day prior to its opening (back then, the state farm show lasted from a Saturday to Friday). So on Friday I drove my yellow rust-bucket of a car, a 1974 Renault 12, through an ice storm on Rt. 283 northwest of Lancaster.

On that day in January 1990, I still feel a steady sweat and watch my knuckles turn white from holding onto the steering wheel for dear life. I could have slid to my death on the four-lane highway at any time.

But I was 29 years old, I thought I have my life before me, it wouldn't end this way and when I arrived, after peeling my hands away from the wheel after the terror ride from Ephrata, Pa. to Harrisburg, I got to my assignment.

I had no idea what I was going to do or what I should do at the swine show. So I asked one gentleman, a 4-H leader and agent by the name of Kenneth Winebark, active in the Lebanon County community. I could never thank Ken enough then, and certainly not now, for instructing me on how to cover a livestock show. He would also be of tremendous assistance during coverage of the Lebanon County fair in late July and early August each year.

Learning how to cover the farming community was hard work. But the events-based newspaper would follow a consistent lineup of show and meeting coverage. You could set your watch to it. The calendar itself, from the beginning of the year to the end, included these "seasons": Farm Show was followed by commodity group meetings season, spring awards banquets, 4-H and FFA events, summer field days, county fairs, Penn State Ag Progress Days (every August), county fairs until late in the fall, banquet/awards season and, at the end, preparations for Farm Show. As I said: clockwork.

At one time in the 1990s, if you just pointed out a date on the calendar, I could tell you, with a high degree of accuracy, what stories we were preparing for the Saturday issue.

The second year of the Farm Show in January 1991 was the same: another ice storm that I drove through, this time I think with my Renault 18i, in much better shape than the rust-bucket R12. I made it there alive and intact. I was a lot better this time at covering the swine shows and maintained a schedule that included three days, with additional sheep shows on Sunday and the state FFA winter convention on Monday — always on Monday.

In 1996, I can remember the FFA winter convention announcement sent to us, indicating, like the postal service, that neither "sleet, rain nor snow" would hinder it. That year the snow was piled up 36 inches high with drifts and, for the first time, the convention was cancelled. The very next year the release came to us with the wording: "The annual winter FFA convention is SCHEDULED...."

(When I returned to the Lancaster Farming office in Ephrata, Pennsylvania in January 1991, the general manager's secretary asked me why, with the inclement weather, I would have covered the event. She was the kind of person, I reminded her carefully, that if I wouldn't have gone, she would have asked me: why not? She simply shrugged and walked away.)

In the years since, before the days of a loaded email inbox and countless things to do as a result of the internet (still about eight years in the future), I was able to put together series of stories on certain farm-related issues. I did several, including series on farm water quality and the dangers of sinkholes, which won statewide newspaper awards.

ESSENTIAL: In the 1990s, as members of what was then called the Pennsylvania Newspaper Publishers Association

(now the Pennsylvania News Media Association), our peers in the field would read and judge our contributions to the annual Keystone Awards, presented to newspaper personnel in conjunction with the association's annual spring meeting. These were the equivalent, statewide, of the newspaper Academy Awards. The importance of peer recognition remains the same: a morale booster, a way to tell your readers that what newspaper staff members write has an impact that matters to the community.

For my work on business features, I won the PennAg Industries Association Agribusiness Journalism of the Year Award in September 1992. I went to the Poconos to receive this significant honor.

A series I wrote for *Lancaster Farming* focused on water quality issues on the farm, sinkhole protection measures, handling farm plastic waste, and many others. The water quality series garnered a second-place award within our division, Division VI, weeklies with more than 45,000 readers. The feature on sinkhole safety garnered an honorable mention. I was proud of these accomplishments and display the awards on my office wall.

I wrote other series as well, including a guide to tree grafting, a series on the history and development of the state Farm Show, including the complex renovations and additions; and many, many others.

Most of the series were finished before a landmark moment when, early in 1998, the staff was assigned to learn the latest in desktop technology, pagination and the world wide web.

Yes, the internet for the farm weekly had arrived.

We began to understand it, slowly. We checked out websites that many companies were creating. This was a boon, initially, because we didn't have to constantly call the local library reference desk for information: we could search for the information. At the time, the computer browser was Netscape. I believe Yahoo was the search engine. I remember checking out the location and information on a field crop research company near Ephrata. Soon we could bookmark many references.

For the company that relied on pink pads to write down messages across all departments, now we had voicemail and email.

With email, we dabbled at first, sending over drafts of stories to the editor (at this time, *Lancaster Farming's* executive editor was Everett Newswanger) or between staff. Most times the information we received was by snail mail and fax machine. Once email began, then my full-time task as editor was email manager, ensuring that all email sent to the weekly farm newspaper went to the right person and the correct department.

At this time, on the internet, many newspapers were beginning to provide copy for free. It was all an effort — and only an effort — to pick up new subscribers.

I will repeat that: copy was given away to entice new subscribers. The thinking by the circulation department was: give away copy so that people would become long-term subscribers.

On our new website at the newspaper, launched in 1999, we would provide access to three top stories. We would then list headlines of other items, only as teasers.

ESSENTIAL: Keep in mind at this time that the only reason why newspapers were giving away free content on their websites was to garner paid PRINT subscribers. That was its only purpose. Nobody thought that newspapers would begin giving away ALL content. Newspapers abandoned the idea of charging for content; after all, weren't paid advertisements supposed to pay the way? Now we have come full circle and most newspapers have installed an aggressive paywall. If you want to read a newspaper today, you have to pay for it, print or digitally.

Paying for newspaper content: what an interesting concept.

One department of *Lancaster Farming* was the mailbox markets. Essentially, subscribers could post, for free in the printed newspaper, ads for items they would want to sell, such as crops, livestock, machinery, etc. That feature alone drew a very loyal readership.

It was at this time the newspaper owners decided that we were going to give away the mailbox markets. That's right, we were offering free content on the web. Advertising was going to carry the weight, right? It didn't matter that the content actually cost money to produce. Giving it away — content readers were happily paying for — was supposed to be the answer to enticing new subscribers.

I was completely against it. Readers wanted to know why we wouldn't give away all our content. I told them I would as soon as Ford started giving away free F150 trucks.

They saw the point.

But my wishes were overridden. Mailbox markets were going to be free, it was that simple, according to the powers-that-be, until things began to change more than a decade later.

ESSENTIAL: Beginning in the mid-2000s, newspapers were still seeking subscribers. The hope was to give away as much copy as possible to garner print subscribers. Many large newspapers did this on a massive scale, so much so that, starting in about 2010, you could read any amount of stories from almost any newspaper for free. After all, print advertising would pay for the newspaper and financially sustain the industry, right? At least editors and publishers believed that. Readers were spoiled. Why should they pay for news when they were so used to receiving it for free? Why subscribe when you don't have to?

I was doing well, for 16-and-a-half years, at Lancaster Farming. The year's activities served as a template for event coverage and days and weeks were consistent and predictable.

However, my career would take a very expansive turn.

I wanted to serve in a bigger capacity. I wanted graduate to "publisher," and the only way I knew how to do that was to get the full experience in publishing, including sales. Besides, the advertising sales professionals I knew could make some great commissions.

Why not expand my own experience in publishing by joining sales? It seemed like a fairly easy career to have. I had the professional contacts, after all.

At one time, Gary Myers, who was advertising director at Lancaster Farming, said I should pursue a career in sales.

So, to get a more full picture of the world of newspaper publishing, I had to expand my scope of experience.

Chapter 8
ACCUSED OF SALES

There was a lot more I needed to learn.

Watching the success of *Lancaster Farming* and how it had grown in readership and advertising sales, I wanted to know a lot more about what makes a publication successful.

So I began to "hybridize" my career.

"Hybridize," you say?

What I mean is that I wanted to experience both ends of the spectrum, including not only editorial but also advertising sales.

Normally in newspapers, editorial handles their own portion of the newspaper and advertising sells ads. It is the classic separation of church (advertising) and state (editorial). It seems like it's the living version of "never the twain shall meet."

I had done quite a bit of selling for my own startup publications, *Philadelphia Computer* and *Entry Magazine*.

You see, there are times that I believe advertising loves me. Or so it seems.

Years ago, when I was a student at Our Mother of Perpetual Help School in Ephrata, Pa., I came in second place two years in a row when I participated in a school fundraiser, selling Christmas decorations and wrap. A few years after that, in public middle school, I came in second place in hoagie sales for the Junior National Honor Society.

(I always landed second place. I wonder if I could place first at some time?)

During the summer months, when I was growing up, my father, Andrew L. Andrews, sold advertising novelty items for the Newton Manufacturing Co. in Newton, Iowa. He continued that in his retirement as a teacher, staying with the company for 40 years and winning many awards for his sales of advertising promotional items. I think Dad often preferred his role as a salesman instead of his career as a teacher.

I would often go on sales trips with Dad in the summer (there was always his treat at an ice cream stand somewhere). I watched how he achieved success by listening well, entertaining his clients with free novelty items (Dad enjoyed giving way free stuff) and asking questions about how they were promoting their place of business. All the while, he was having fun and his clients knew that. They could see he genuinely enjoyed what he was doing.

Dieter Krieg, publisher and editor of *Farmshine* (the country's only weekly dairy industry newspaper), gave my career a "restart" as a freelance salesperson in 2006. I have not thanked him nearly enough for his kindness. My first pure sales experience was the August event for farmers in

Pennsylvania, Penn State's annual Ag Progress Days near State College, in early August 2006.

I sold an ad for Farmshine on the first day. And I picked up several more new clients, brand-new to Farmshine.

I was on my way to a successful career in sales.

Again, I recalled what Gary Myers, former advertising director for *Lancaster Farming*, said to me one day: "Andy, you would do well in sales."

So I took Gary for his word and set off to be an ad salesperson for the next eight years.

I can remember some of the basic training I endured on the job with my own startup publications. Don't be afraid to reach out (it is, after all, a numbers game). Listen carefully. Try to find out what works and what doesn't for a potential client. Contact them not five times, but 30 times if you have to. Make sure they are aware of the brand. Make sure you deliver a good return on investment for them.

The first ad I sold in my eight-year career as a salesman was for a fly-control company for the dairy industry when I was a freelance ad sales representative for *Farmshine* newspaper in August 2006. After that, I secured a high-frequency advertiser in *Farmshine* for a steel storage structure company out of Canada. Many other new advertisers followed.

My sales and writing (see, a hybrid even then!) for *Farmshine* went well and Dieter Krieg, the publisher and editor, always treated me with kindness and respect. To this day, we have a great relationship.

In the eight years of experience in sales, my No. 1 priority — probably my own downfall — was an obsession with obtaining brand-new clients. Always. I would call and reach out very aggressively to prospects that should be taking advantage of the selected, targeted reach newspapers could provide. Of course, at this time, the newspaper I worked for was a trade journal.

ESSENTIAL: Whether it is a weekly community newspaper, a daily or a trade journal, I believe in the high value of print. For one thing, a newspaper is self-contained: it has all the editorial and advertisements that are trending and are paramount to loyal readers. Honestly, do you see ALL content a newspaper has online? There is a certain amount of professional experience, trust, brand dependability and feedback a newspaper delivers that often can't be provided in one package, by itself, online to a targeted audience. Newspapers have always been a source for many successful businesses. Always.

I had to make a move that made sense: work for an industry that is immune to the ups and downs, the boom times and recessions, of the regular economy, in order to have some sense of job security. What economy is that, you wonder?

The "Medicaid Economy," of course.

A large part of the Medicaid Economy is senior health, housing and other services. Those services only grow year by year, despite a recession. While the general economy may sometimes stammer and fall, the Medicaid Economy just continues to grow.

In August 2007, I saw an employment advertisement from the publisher of *Senior News*, On-Line Publishing, from Columbia, Pa. that made sense. At least I could learn about a new industry at a time, right before the start of the 2008-2010 Great Recession, which seemed unaffected. It came at the most opportune moment: September 2007, right before the start of the Great Recession.

I was beginning to learn a lot about the important role of advertising sales and to continue my "hybridization" as a writer and ad salesperson.

I realized at this point that I could do both: write for a newspaper and sell advertising. And do both really well.

I continued to contribute features and coverage of events to Farmshine while I was employed at the *Senior News*. At the time, for On-Line Publishing, I was territorial advertising representative for Lebanon and Chester counties.

Donna Anderson is publisher of the senior newspapers, with separate editions devoted to Lancaster, Lebanon, Dauphin, Cumberland, York and Chester counties. A large part of her success could be attributed to the company's senior expos, day events conducted in different counties at certain times of the year, to draw seniors from long-term care facilities, assisted living, independent living and in-home living throughout the region.

At one time during the Great Recession of 2009, the Anderson family decided to revive a Columbia, Pa. weekly newspaper called the *Columbia Register*. While advertisers were initially committed to its success, they backed out of contracts and the publishers could no longer afford to print it. I believe it lasted about nine months before ceasing publication by early 2010.

Newspapers at this time were under threat. Advertising dropped dramatically low as a result of the mortgage-backed securities financial disaster happening around the globe, and the economy, with far too many people bludgeoned by too much debt, losing their jobs.

I remember at the very beginning of the Great Recession of 2007-2008, On-Line Publishers launched *"b" Magazine* for the boomer generation. We celebrated when the publication was launched in February 2008. Little did we know that at the end of the year, the Great Recession would be felt by millions of workers and businesses as retail and restaurant advertising dropped. It was the worst economic downturn since the Great Depression of the 1930s, and it felt, literally, like the Great Depression II.

What was happening to newspapers at the time?

In June 2009, the last edition of the *Lancaster New Era* was published. It was combined with the morning edition of the *Lancaster Intelligencer Journal* that same year.

Seven years before, the *Reading Times*, the morning edition in Reading, Pennsylvania was combined with the afternoon *Reading Eagle*. The *Reading Eagle* became a morning edition.

More about the *Reading Eagle*, later.

For now, beside massive consolidations of morning and afternoon editions at newspapers around the country, what else was happening?

The March 18, 2009 edition of *Editor & Publisher* cited the move by big business to begin to acquire struggling dailies. And a story quotes the Newspaper Association of America when it noted that ad revenue fell 23% in 2008. A combination of sell-offs, too much debt, Craigslist and the fall-off in classified revenue spelled doom for many newspapers.

I needed to make a change and to find something closer to home.

That's when the *Harrisburg Patriot-News* came into my life.

As I joined as the outer territory sales representative for the Harrisburg *Patriot-News* in 2011, which at the beginning of 2013 would change its name to the PA Media Group and reorganize as a company with digital reach as a No. 1 priority. At the time, then-24-year old reporter Sara Ganim became one of the youngest reporters in history to win the Pulitzer Prize (in local reporting) for breaking a story that a grand jury was investigating the sexual abuse scandal at Penn State University involving Penn State Assistant Football Coach Jerry Sandusky. I was watching what was happening very closely to see what affect winning a Pulitzer would have on newspaper ad revenue and circulation.

Not much, sadly.

When I joined the *Patriot-News* in late 2011 as an ad salesman, newspapers began a steep, steady decline. In late 2012, the *Patriot-News* was reforming and renaming itself. The newspaper, witnessing more declines in paid advertising than it could handle, particularly for the Friday, Saturday, Monday and Wednesday editions, went to a three-time-per week format, published instead on Sundays, Tuesdays and Thursdays.

Advance Publications, owners of the *Patriot-News*, renamed the operation PA Media Group. The focus: digital would be a primary business operation. Instead of selling print ads with impressions on the PennLive website, we would be part of a digital ad agency selling primarily behavior-targeted digital display and search engine advertising. Everything went from special issue advertising to targeted behavioral marketing.

I still had responsibilities for some specialty print products, including the *Central PA Magazine*, part of the promotional arm of the local PBS affiliate, WITF TV. There was a senior publication called *NOW* and a health magazine, *Body and Mind*. But the company was laser-focused on increasing digital advertising.

I did all of that successfully during the transition to a digital-foremost philosophy beginning in early 2013 and lasting until late 2014. I was meeting and exceeding goals for advertising. I placed dozens of new digital advertising clients. The *Patriot-News* survived the transition: I was part of a three-member "legacy team" from what *Patriot-News* was all about originally and became a digital targeting specialist. Their technicians and targeting specialists are the best.

ESSENTIAL: Based on my in-the-trenches sales analysis, at the time, having won the Pulitzer Award for the Sandusky controversy gave the **Harrisburg Patriot-News** ***a slight uptick in subscriptions. Winning a Pulitzer is tough to monetize in terms of advertising sales. As an ad representative, while we***

received lots of extra publicity from a host of other news organizations such as television and radio, there was little to show for it in terms of advertising dollars. However, the online PennLive had a great deal more page views than before the Pulitzer Prize was awarded. Winning awards often cannot be directly monetized, unfortunately.

While successful at what I was doing, I still felt empty about my accomplishments.

I hit an impasse — emotionally and mentally — in my career. With painstaking work, I had built up numerous proposals for potential new advertisers. I carefully researched their business. I asked a lot of questions. I analyzed how they get customers, and where. I built up arrays of spec ads and plans for digital targeting that were reviewed by our technicians. I was careful and meticulous. I composed dozens (actually, a total of 171) new proposals, each carefully put together by information they provided to us during the discovery process.

I looked over the file one day of the 171 PowerPoint proposals and they were solid. The spec ads created fit their concepts and needs.

And nobody was buying. Suddenly I had a sinking feeling in my stomach when I calculated how much time was lost in composing 171 different proposals, and days of work, that went nowhere.

I thought about my previous life and work in editorial. I couldn't think of any moment that I was rejected — told NO — 171 different times.

By going to the three-times-per-week publication schedule, I was shocked. What was going to happen to the "lifestyle" readers, the ones who picked up a copy at a local convenience store with their cup of coffee? Or who picked up the day's issue in the break room?

How about the-not-so-technological-savvy readers who demanded a print version that they wouldn't have to "print out"? Who was going to look after the lifestyle readers, who for decades have looked forward to "their" paper on their doorstep.

What of them?

What of me?

So at the top of my game in advertising, when my goals were met and I was exceeding advertising goals, I made the decision. It would be now or never. I responded to an Indeed advertisement to join a local, family owned, community DAILY newspaper, the *Reading Eagle*.

Meanwhile, I wanted to take what I learned about specialty publications and what they meant to a higher level with a 150-year-old family newspaper that was recognized by the state newspaper and other media association as the best community newspaper in the state.

Separation of Church and State

In the four decades I have worked for professional publishers, one thing I have come to recognize are the deep-seated feelings both editorial and advertising have for what they should be doing, or not doing.

Since I have worked on both sides of "The Wall" between those departments, a separation that remains in place for a variety of reasons, I have formed my own conclusions.

The argument goes something like this:

Editorial believes it is unethical for advertising to place pressure on how news is covered and written, and large advertisers — those who spend a lot of money in the newspaper — should not, because of their role in the business of the newspaper, influence how and when news is published. Editorial believes in that separation created by The Wall: neither side shall influence the other. Editorial shouldn't kowtow to the whims of advertisers. Advertisers should not insist that they be "covered" by any news reporting and gain an upper hand in the management of the newsroom.

Advertising believes that because they are the bread and butter for the newspaper, with their work influencing salaries and overall business goals for the news organization, that they should be represented and their clients should have a say in coverage, especially when news hits close to their industry. Because of the investment that advertisers make in the success of the news organization, ad directors believe clients need and deserve their fair share of mention in the newspaper when appropriate, such as news stories that delve into certain industries advertisers represent.

So The Wall exists. The unwritten, unmandated, generally accepted rule is: Neither shall cross The Wall. Editorial should not influence advertising or be influenced by it. Advertising wants representation because of the business investment they make in the news enterprise.

Editorial remains adamant about The Wall.

Advertising sometimes wants The Wall to be either taken down, or remain somewhat tentative, or flexible.

But the advertising colleagues I know realize how important it is to maintain the separation created by The Wall and do go out of their way to be sure there is news integrity and make no promises of editorial coverage to their clients. At least that is what I have seen in my career as both newspaper reporter and editor and as an advertising professional.

The point I am making, if newspapers want to be successful, is to ensure The Wall remains. And keep it intact.

But, I have one caveat: if possible, when writing business features on certain industries, home fashion trends or articles on new vehicle development, and such, it wouldn't hurt to reach out to the advertisers. I believe if they receive that contact, their likelihood of continuing in their major role as advertisers can continue.

But in this era of the coronavirus — in the days of a continuing struggle with digital display ads and search advertising consuming print budgets across the entire industry — we need to look at The Wall a little more closely, a bit more thoroughly.

Why? Because more print-only clients are being assaulted by the digital search representatives, cable companies, behavior-targeting agencies and others. There is terrible strain on print advertising budgets.

When I was in print advertising at the Patriot-News, I remember in one of our many training sessions that one of our instructors said to obtain advertising for any commodity or project, you have to "steal" it from somewhere else. That same stealing works the other way: after all, Google took away billions of dollars in advertising that used to go to newspapers.

Because of this strain, if newspapers are to survive, they must do this:

- Remind advertisers that newspapers are a "showcase" for products and services. They are an educational tool. Those are things Google and Bing searches cannot accomplish.
- Engage the advertisers in providing that form of education in the special sections provided. These sections on health, aging, gardening, home improvement and education can provide a complete showcase of services that can't be found on Google, Bing or Facebook.
- Work with special section editors to determine a plan for engagement.

ESSENTIAL: "Engagement" of advertisers, through the use of special sections, allow them to educate the readers about what products and services they offer. This outlet allows them representation in features focusing on the industry.

- Special-section editors should allow room for this engagement by promoting education-specific columns that allow advertisers a chance to reach out to new customers and the columns should provide a contact source to put advertisers directly in front of readers.

There has to be engagement of advertisers far beyond the print advertising they do. The one weapon they have against search advertising is the ability to showcase products and services: that can't be done on search or social media. There are limits to the reach an ad message conveys, especially on the limits with social media.

If newspapers are to survive, then engagement is the word they need to learn.

Digital? No

If advertisers are used to circulation that runs from 15,000 to 70,000 daily subscribers in print form, some critics believe that asking all former print subscribers to go online could be asking too much.

I think it's too much because, partially, so many people, subscribing to many local and national news services, are essentially getting a lot of news for free. We've spoiled former newsprint readers that way: since the 2000s, organizations gave away a lot of editorial to boost print subscribers. So for two decades, we've conditioned people to get their news for free.

I know of one newspaper with a circulation of about 15,000 but about 4,000 digital subscribers. That is excellent! Read Chapter 16 for more details of why one community newspaper has been so successful.

Chapter 9
RETURN OF THE MAN

Return of the Mack (Oh my God)
You know that I'll be back (Here I am)

— "Return of the Mack"
by Mark Morrison

I enjoyed my work for LNP Weeklies quite a bit. I loved the camaraderie and friendships that I created. I enjoyed the products we published.

I kept thinking how well I was able to survive more than a decade and a half of working on a weekly newspaper, and how I thrived in that environment. I loved the work; and I started to think it was time to see if I could return to it.

After avoiding daily newspapers for fear of the frustration of daily deadlines, why did I want to return?

At the Patriot-News, while the work was steady and I was always meeting or exceeding advertising sales goals. I was cold-calling a lot and setting up appointments for new advertisers, with new potential digital and print campaigns, left and right. Income was steady and bonuses arrived, fairly consistently; so I was content.

At one time, a fairly large and new business opened up south of Lancaster city, my territory. They were a heavily capitalized startup. I won't name them, because I think the work to perhaps capture their advertising business is still underway, but at the time, I put a lot of effort into a discovery and proposal for them.

Keep in mind that a discovery meeting is very exhaustive. You ask a lot of questions about a business: how they began, what they make, how much it cost them to make it, how they promote the product or service, what has worked or failed with past promotions, what their audience is, who their buyers are, how they obtain buyers and focus in on what the formula for their advertising success would be.

Then you have to examine the data collected and work with the digital experts, and the *Patriot-News* organization (the PA Media Group) had quite a few of them. They would comb through a proposal that I put together that addresses what the client said they wanted and what tools we were going to use to deliver them potential sales leads. (After all, we couldn't increase their sales; our duty was to find potential customers, and I had to carefully explain to them that's all we did.)

Then there are revisions to the PowerPoint proposal. Sometimes many revisions. The numbers have to be just right.

When the day came to present the proposal, the package was complete, including spec digital ads and other return-on-investment items and calculations. This was a solid, pragmatic proposal for where the business was at the time.

In mid-June 2014, I submitted the proposal for a combination of search-engine marketing and behavior-targeted digital display advertising, along with some search engine optimization with the Lancaster company's website. The total package would cost the company about $8,000 per month.

If the company accepted this proposal, I would make all my digital goals for a full year, from the September 2014 launch until September 2015, with another proposal in the works to renew.

There was a team of four of us, including my boss at the time, Dave Liperote; a web expert; a behavior-targeting expert; and a marketing manager.

Let's put it this way: if this proposal, which literally put my career in the balance, would have been accepted, the chances of me leaving the PA Media Group would have been very, very slim.

In early September, after the deadline came and there was no contract, I looked into my file cabinet. There were dozens of near-perfect proposals filled with spec ads and calculations that were all carefully reviewed. I mean dozens.

Why didn't they succeed? There could be a variety of reasons. Perhaps the proposal targeted spend was too high. Perhaps (at least in several cases) the advertising budget for the client changed, dramatically. Or it could be that the client was not sure of our branding. I'm not sure.

I shop in Lancaster occasionally as part of my travels, and I did the same when I was at PA Media Group. One night I was picking up groceries, in late August, in the

Stauffers of Rohrerstown, near Lancaster, Pa., when the public address system was playing a background song. I was listening to the lyrics about "running up that road, running up that hill," and the song was lyrical and emotional. I thought, gee, that is me in this position, with proposals that were carefully researched and written, going nowhere.

Then I thought, maybe it's time to change. Time to find something to do elsewhere. A change of career.

I did a search of those lyrics and came across the song from 1985 by Kate Bush, "Running Up That Hill (A Deal With God)." And these lyrics:

And if I only could
I'd make a deal with God
And I'd get him to swap our places
I'd be running up that road
Be running up that hill
With no problems

If I stopped running up that road, that hill, chasing new advertisers, I would find happiness.

That seemed safe enough.

I needed to make a drastic change in my career. Anything was better than listening to another "no" from a potential advertiser.

I had submitted my resume several times to Editor Harry Deitz at the *Reading Eagle* whenever there was a need for a reporter or editor, and was turned down every time.

I submitted my resume to Deitz again in late August, after learning that my major ad proposal at the PA Media Group was turned down.

I late August of 2014, I submitted my resume again. I was qualified for what the newspaper was seeking: an experienced, award-winning business editor for the newspaper's *Business Weekly* publication. After all, that's what I did as editor of *Lancaster Farming*, with agribusinesses.

I missed the joys and rewards of working with staff and correspondents. I missed the creative sections and ideas the staff of the farm newspaper would generate. I missed the companionship of my peers and colleagues.

In September 2014, Deitz finally called me in for an interview in the afternoon of Sept. 11 with the *Reading Eagle* for the position of business editor for the newspaper. At last! I wanted to return to editorial after an eight-year hiatus. Because of my experiences at Lancaster County Weeklies (*Lancaster Farming*), I thought it was a good fit. And so in early October 2014, I accepted the job as editor of the weekly business tabloid publication, *Business Weekly*, and business editor at the *Reading Eagle*.

It was a fantastic experience. I would manage three full-time writer/contributors and access to about a dozen correspondents. Some of the highlight issues included the Economic Outlook issue in May, the top Berks County employers edition and quite a few more special editions I helped put together, including Women in Business and the Young Professionals issues.

So at the top of my game in advertising, when my goals were met and I was exceeding advertising goals, I made the decision: It would be now or never. I responded to an Indeed advertisement to join a local, family owned, community DAILY newspaper, the* Reading Eagle. *(Photo by Tim Leedy,* Reading Eagle*)

I adopted a model developed by Lancaster Newspapers in 1989: themed special sections. I expanded the weekly publication's editorial calendar, expanding from 25 weeks of the year for special themed editions to every week.

It has to do with a business model that I saw in action both in my work at the Lancaster County Weeklies in editorial and at the *Patriot-News* in advertising: concentrating on a certain theme for select sections.

It's all about what "Perceived Value, Justified Expense."

"Perceived Value" is the notion, for instance, that if you are an accounting business, and a weekly business publication is featuring a specially themed issue about accounting, readers can focus in on what you do. If you need to get approval from the bosses for a media buy, or are working for a media buyer, going into the themed issue is a "Justified Expense." It just makes sense to showcase/promote/advertise your business in a themed issue that focuses on your business. The model is simple and has worked since at least the late 1980s.

It was fairly easy to report about regional business news and highlight business-to-business developments while creating compelling copy to help business succeed.

A warning about using this model: using a theme model for special sections takes a higher degree of creativity, content management, planning and execution. But if you want to see a dramatic increase in advertising revenue and reader engagement, you would be hard-put to come up with a better plan.

ESSENTIAL: Ad revenue blossomed with themed specialty issues because, combined with a focus on local businesses and those who consider themselves thought-leaders in the featured field, readership engagement skyrocketed and ad revenue went up dramatically. Sure, it takes a lot of planning to provide compelling copy on themed issues. But it can be done. It is a lot of extra work and requires great

communication, but it was successful for 13 years at* Lancaster Farming *and provided dramatic revenue growth from 1993 to 2006 and beyond, and three years for the* Reading Eagle Business Weekly *from 2014 through 2017. And special section ad revenue grew dramatically for the special sections from 2018 through 2020, until the pandemic hit. Yet I continues to drive newspaper ad revenue.

At the time, I thought it was simply a great working model. Today it may be the only way for newspapers to survive, by becoming more creative with special, themed sections.

In October 2017 I was asked to expand the themed-issue ideas for a bunch of special sections that were business-to-consumer-oriented, including *Reading Eagle's Health & Wellness, 50 Plus, Home & Garden, Bridal Showcase* and others. The reasoning, I am sure, had to deal with the explosive growth of the *Business Weekly* section, which doubled its ad income from 2015 to 2017.

Perhaps I could convey the same success with my editorial formula to ALL the *Reading Eagle* special sections?

Let me backtrack for just a minute again and talk about the real origins of special sections.

The key to today's newspaper survival actually began in the late 1980s. In my experience, it began with the newspapers in southeast Pennsylvania, especially Lancaster Newspapers in Lancaster, when readers began to see home improvement special sections. It came home with the annual summer "progress" special sections that looked at the community business makeup each year. It included the spring and fall home and garden sections, health and fitness sections, senior-care and aging population sections. And the special newspaper sections worked, especially when the sections contained, almost entirely, local content.

The key to newspaper survival? Exclusively local content. But more so: what I call DIRECTED CONTENT. If you want an opinion that could be published and could point the way to advertising, allow the businesses to participate in a special column or focus on a trend in a purely educational way, in a specially themed section. Writers should speak to businesses in the theme when developing a story angle. Most importantly, special themes that are laser-focused on specific businesses can involve and engage them, where they desire to be a part of the section. Allow the businesses to offer their opinions on developments and trends. Network and engage the community PERSONALLY. As an editor, I would speak about the sections at network meetings. News travels fast.

That is the model! LNP and other newspapers became wildly successful with this model and they stuck with this plan for years, in all their print enterprises. And it worked. It requires a higher level of management of special publications and a lot more foresight and planning, but it provides the key elements of selling today's newspapers: "Perceived Value Equals Justified Spend."

> *Perceived Value: Small companies and their media buyers, either in house or contracted through an advertising agency, have limited promotional budgets. They are going to be very selective when spending ad dollars. If you are a business publication and the "theme" for the upcoming issue is accounting and investments, for example, similar companies are*

going to perceive a higher value for that specific issue than just the normal "run-of-press," called ROP, insertion in a publication. There is fear businesses may have that their competitors will be included and will grab a share of the shrinking market. So the ad value is strong.

Justified Spend: Media buyers need to maximize their advertising dollars. They must go to their decision-makers to advertise in a specially themed issue. It is much easier to justify the spend if the issue will focus on the critical aspects of running a type of business, say, in accounting. The ad buyer took a calculated risk with a dwindling advertising budget in a smart way and obtains good return on investment, with call-to-action advertising, or, in brand (image) advertising, to keep their business top of mind for readers.

Cautious About Debt

The formula works to sustain a good community newspaper. But these newspapers have to be very, very cautious about how much debt they can take on.

However, there was a darkness to the past of the *Reading Eagle*. Inexplicably, with no established path to revenue, the company decided to invest about $37 million in a new Berliner web printing press and custom press building. This happened in 2009, the beginning of an era in which the tried-and-true newspaper industry was being heavily challenged by a terrible Great Recession. I suppose they thought if a new building would be built, and a new press installed, income would come.

But the decision to take on debt to pay for the press and building was a financial albatross. It placed the Reading Eagle Company in heavy debt. Subsequently, the company defaulted on a loan from a major bank to the tune of $25 million.

What was going on? I was dimly aware since 2014 of the cost of the new press and building the *Reading Eagle* installed. I knew there was a lot of consternation about justifying its cost. There were layoffs. This I had come to expect, having seen what happened to other newspapers from 2009 to 2013.

But at the family-owned Eagle? How could this happen?

On the first day of spring in 2019, the family-owned business that has published the Reading Eagle newspaper for more than 150 years filed for bankruptcy protection.

Writer David Mekeel provided very transparent reporting of the crisis the newspaper was enduring.

Here's Mekeel's report from the *Reading Eagle*:

> *The company will continue to publish and broadcast under Chapter 11 bankruptcy rules, while it seeks a buyer to take over the Eagle's news and broadcasting legacy, company officials said.*
>
> *"For more than a century you have taken us into your homes and supported us as we've told your stories and reported on the events and policies that shape your lives," the company says in a note to readers.*

"We hope you will stay with us as we move through this period of change."

At a meeting with employees late this afternoon, company President and CEO Peter D. Barbey said the company is pursuing options for the future with other news media companies. The company has 236 full-time employees and 20 part-time.

He applauded employees, many of whom have spent their careers with the company, for their dedication and work that has earned the company scores of state, national and international awards in the last decade, including a 2018 Newspaper of the Year honor from the Pennsylvania NewsMedia Association.

"Our employees have worked very hard to support our company and our community," Barbey said. "The family is incredibly grateful."

The company retained a media broker, Dirks, Van Essen, Murray & April, and has met with several potential buyers over the past few months. The company is hopeful that its position as the top provider of local news will attract a buyer with the commitment and resources to move the business forward and serve the community well.

Reading Eagle is the single most-used source of local news and information in the market among all demographics, according to a 2016 Nielsen market survey.

The Reading Eagle has an average daily circulation of more than 37,000 Monday through Friday, and more than 50,000 on Sunday, according to the company. Its companion website, readingeagle.com, averages more than 600,000 unique users and 3.2 million pageviews a month.

The weekly South Schuylkill News reaches some 2,800 households in southern Schuylkill County. WEEU, a news/talk station that broadcasts at 830 on the AM dial, has 20,000 watts of power in the daytime, and 6,000 at night.

The first Daily Reading Eagle was published on Jan. 28, 1868 by Ritter & Co., a partnership of William S. Ritter and Jesse G. Hawley, husband of Kate E. Ritter. Reading Eagle Company was incorporated in 1904. The company acquired the Reading Times in 1940 and WEEU radio in 1946. The Reading Times ceased publication in 2002 and the Reading Eagle became the morning newspaper. In 2009, the Reading Eagle began publication on its new press, a 77,000-square-foot addition to its facility at 345 Penn St., rear.

The media leaders and decision-makers thought that print remained king and wanted to live perpetually in the 1980s and 1990s, before the internet changed the makeup of all business, especially print media. They were relying on the belief that perhaps, if you built a new press, business would come. They thought a new press would result in more income. Little did they know that, fundamentally, it was getting harder to turn a daily community newspaper into a moneymaking enterprise that could afford $37 million of debt.

Unfortunately, a confluence of bad business decisions forced the inevitable bankruptcy and sale of the *Reading Eagle*, the longest same-family-owned newspaper in the U.S., if not the world.

From the March 22, 2019 Reading Eagle, in a story written by David Mekeel:

> *The troubles began in 2009 when the company took on a "substantial debt" to complete a 77,000-square-foot expansion of its 345 Penn St. headquarters. The space was created to house a new press and consolidated distribution center.*
>
> *But a pattern of declining advertising revenue made the debt hard to pay back.*
>
> *Between 2016 and 2018, the documents report, the company's advertising revenue dropped from $17 million to $12.6 million.*
>
> *The rapid loss of advertising revenue, in turn, led to deteriorating earnings before interest, taxes, depreciation and amortization (EBITDA), a common benchmark for the performance of a business.*
>
> *That EBITDA number went from minus $916,000 on sales of $35.2 million in 2016 to minus $4 million on sales of $28 million in 2018.*
>
> *The company's financial problems caused it to default in 2009 on the loan from Sovereign Bank. At the time*

of the default, the company owed the bank about $25 million.

In 2016, facing foreclosure by Santander Bank, formerly Sovereign Bank, on the loan, Reading Eagle Company President and Chief Executive Officer Peter D. Barbey bought the company's debt from the bank. The purchase was made through BWH Media LLC, a subsidiary of Barbey's Black Walnut Holdings LLC.

After the purchase of the debt by BWH Media, Reading Eagle Company continued to operate at a significant cash flow loss. That led BWH Media to provide additional loans to the company, averaging about $250,000 a month. Those loans were added to the debt bought from Santander Bank.

The company took steps to try to stabilize the business, including layoffs. Those moves were countered by increasing costs for things such as newsprint. At the same time, revenue continued to decline.

The court documents say the only way costs can be further decreased is through further cuts to the newsroom, which "cannot bear millions of dollars of cuts."

"Unfortunately, it has now become apparent to the debtors and Mr. Barbey that, despite their best efforts, the debtors are no longer a sustainable stand-alone business under the current structure," one of the documents reads.

Court documents list the company's assets at just over $15 million and its liabilities at just under $38.5 million.

According to the *Reading Eagle*, from 2019, which remained transparent throughout the Chapter 11 bankruptcy process:

Late in March, the company filed paperwork in federal court officially seeking bankruptcy protection.

Employees were gathered inside a third-floor meeting room Wednesday afternoon, just before the paperwork was submitted, to hear a short announcement by (owner Peter) Barbey about the decision.

In general, to declare bankruptcy means the amount of one's debts is more than its assets and income can support, and there are no immediate prospects of paying those debts off in a timely manner.

A Chapter 11 bankruptcy — meaning it is filed under Chapter 11 of the U.S. Bankruptcy Code — is often referred to as a "reorganization" bankruptcy and is used by a business to reorganize its debt under the protection of the bankruptcy court.

Beforehand, meanwhile, I was moved from my title of business editor (October 2014 to October 2017) to special sections editor (October 2017 to April 2020).

It was critical to remain profitable. We doubled the profitability of *Business Weekly* from 2015 to 2017. How? I was able to add special themed issues to every week of the weekly business publication, involve a lot more columnists, expand our network by involvement in all the major business networking groups, forge alliances with more in-county and bordering county chambers of commerce and engage readers whenever I could.

Here's a cover from one of the editions of Business Weekly *in the* Reading Eagle.

I became the longest editor in *Business Weekly's* history (and still am).

At the same time, the *Reading Eagle* continued to win the sweepstakes award in Division II (newspapers from about 30,000 to 75,000 daily readers) for best community newspaper. The newspaper was named winner of the 2018 and 2019 Pennsylvania Newsmedia Association community newspaper of the year award.

So the readers loved the newspaper and saw the value. Advertisers purchased ads. Income doubled on not only on the business section but the other sections I was able to lead.

All went well until the March 2019 bankruptcy. A new owner took over. Today, the newspaper is part of the Alden mutual fund group through MediaNews Group. That group owns most of the daily newspapers throughout southeast Pennsylvania and many other newspapers across the country.

The media chain owns the *San Jose Mercury News*, *The Denver Post*, *The Boston Herald*, *St. Paul Pioneer Press* and the *San Jose Mercury News*.

In early April, the business cut 19 staff positions, including mine, all because of the coronavirus pandemic.

Breaking-News Update

Several days before this book went to press in late November 2020, we learned this:

From the *Reading Eagle*:

The former Reading Eagle Company building at 345 Penn St. is under a sale agreement, said NAI Keystone real estate agent Steve Willems.

Willems could not discuss any other details, including the potential sale price and buyer, because the property is under contract.

Philadelphia-based iPM Assist, a virtual construction project management company, posted on Instagram that it was excited to "manage the remodel" and the building will receive an exterior facelift.

The post said the "inside will house several retailers, a marketplace, restaurant, office space and so much more. We envision this building to be a hub for networking and creativity."

Aris Degirmenci, a project manager with iPM Assist, confirmed the company would be overseeing the project.

Degirmenci and iPM Assist are also overseeing the renovation of the Madison Building at 400 Washington St.

The 105,874-square-foot Eagle building was originally listed for $3.25 million in October 2019.

MediaNews Group, a Denver, Colo.-based company that owns 97 publications across the country, purchased the assets of Reading Eagle Company for $5 million and began operating the newspaper July 1, 2019.

Reading Eagle Company filed for Chapter 11 federal bankruptcy protection March 20, 2019, citing an untenable financial situation.

When the building went up for sale last year, Edward Condra, MediaNews Group senior publisher, said Reading Eagle employees and offices will remain at 345 Penn St.

"We are reducing our footprint by relocating employees to the Penn Street side of the building," Condra said.

Condra on Tuesday night said he is aware that there is an agreement of sale.

"At this point we don't know the potential new owner's intentions for the space," he said. "If a sale is finalized, regardless, we plan to have an office in the Reading market."

Chapter 10
WHAT WENT WRONG?

Even before COVID-19, newspapers were struggling to stay open. Quite a few had already closed. If they were purchased, it was usually by a media conglomerate, which immediately began to dismantle it, or at least change it in ways many readers and advertisers didn't agree with.

The *Reading Eagle* was purchased by MediaNews Group in July 2019 and almost immediately there were many changes for one bid of $5 million. It was the only bid.

But many in the media questioned what happened to the 151-year-old family newspaper.

From the June 11, 2010 *Washington Post* about the new owners and executives, including Heath Freeman, of the *Reading Eagle*:

> *Ask Heath Freeman why he got into the newspaper business and the explanation is specific and bloodless.*
>
> *It was 2009, and the Great Recession was forcing many major newspaper chains into bankruptcy. Freeman was a finance guy in New York, still in his 20s, with a sports-bro patter about his days as a*

place-kicker at Duke and an eagerness to make his mark. He looked at some spreadsheets, decided that media execs didn't know what they were doing — and started making some purchases.

"We saw an opportunity," Freeman told The Washington Post, "to help fix the broken model."

Pretty soon, Freeman's firm, Alden Global Capital, had gained control of MediaNews Group, owner of more than 50 papers including the Pulitzer-winning Denver Post, St. Paul Pioneer Press *and the* San Jose Mercury News. *And he was just getting started.*

The current era has been rough for the entire newspaper industry, hit by collapses in both ad revenue and circulation, missteps in the move to digital publication and competition from Web platforms for the remaining readers and advertisers. In the decade-plus Alden has been in the newspaper industry, the number of employees at U.S. newspapers has been cut in half, according to Pew Research Center. But Alden's cuts have been far deeper — more than 70 percent of unionized staff, according to data from the Communications Workers of America union — and its circulation losses steeper, according to Alliance for Audited Media.

He wants it to be understood that he's neither a nonprofit manager nor a billionaire philanthropist. In conversations with friends, he has complained that many of the industry's actual billionaires escape the scrutiny he's received — such as Peter Barbey, a Pennsylvania retail heir who sold the Reading Eagle

> *to Alden's MediaNews and also bought and shuttered the legendary* Village Voice.

Here's a story from the July 10, 2020 *New York Times*, written by Dan Barry, that talks about one reporter's role, the *Pottstown Mercury's* Evan Brandt, in finding the story about the future of newspapers under Alden's MediaNews Group:

> *But they are an endangered species being nudged toward extinction by the most important news story in decades. The coronavirus.*
>
> *The economic paralysis caused by the pandemic has clobbered a newspaper industry already on the mat. With revenues plummeting, substantial layoffs, furloughs and pay reductions have followed in newsrooms across the country.*
>
> *Meanwhile, the hedge funds and private equity firms that own many newspapers often siphon away profits rather than reinvest in local journalism. Frequently associated with this business model is the Alden Global Capital hedge fund, which controls the* Mercury*, Mr. Brandt's employer for 23 years.*
>
> *Mr. Brandt visited the Long Island home of Heath Freeman, the president of Alden Global Capital.*

Unannounced, Brandt visited Freeman's home and caught the executive by surprise. Brandt's simple question was: is the hedge fund group committed to the survival of local journalism? Barry's story noted there was no answer given.

But what about digital advertising? Isn't that what killed newspapers? Or was it a failure to adopt a model that was more engaging to local readers and advertisers?

ESSENTIAL: What search engines and social media sites don't do are provide an ADVERTISING SHOWCASE, such as print advertisements do. In other words, how can search and social media truly SHOWCASE the products and services of a company? Many times we learn about products and services from businesses by seeing an advertisement. You can get a good feeling about exactly what a business has, and how it operates, by viewing display ads in newspapers. This has not been replaced by search and social media, fortunately.

In 1990, newspapers were king, according to journalism.org. Daily newspaper average circulation throughout the country was 63 million, the same for Sunday editions. That was the best year from 1940 until the present day.

Things changed. According to journalism.org:

> *The estimated total U.S. daily newspaper circulation (print and digital combined) in 2018 was 28.6 million for weekday and 30.8 million for Sunday, down 8% and 9%, respectively, from the previous year.*
>
> *Weekday print circulation decreased 12% and Sunday print circulation decreased 13%.*

Digital circulation is harder to judge, according to the website:

Gauging digital audience for the entire newspaper industry is difficult since many daily newspapers do not receive enough traffic to their websites to be measured by Comscore, the data source relied on here. Thus, the figures offered above reflect the top 50 U.S. daily newspapers based on circulation. In the fourth quarter of 2018, there was an average of 11.6 million monthly unique visitors (across all devices) for these top 50 newspapers. This is nearly the same as in Q4 2017 (11.5 million) and 2016 (11.7 million); following two years of growth from 2014 to 2016, newspapers' website traffic has leveled off. (The list of top 50 papers is based on Sunday circulation but also includes The Wall Street Journal, *which does not report Sunday circulation to AAM. It also includes* The Washington Post *and* The New York Times, *which make the top 50 even though they do not fully report their digital circulation to AAM.*

In 2018, only 35 percent of all newspaper advertising came from digital, according to journalism.org.

According to journalism.org, U.S. newsroom employment has dropped a quarter since 2008, with the largest decline in July of 2019. That date corresponds to a time that I was certain I was going to be laid off at the *Reading Eagle.* The new owners picked me up as special sections editor, but only for nine months.

Despite the heavy declines, newspaper print readership remains. Why? Because strictly print readership sometimes represents an older audience and aging demographics.

The aging demographics show a preference for print. Retirees can enjoy their favorite newspaper along with their morning coffee on their favorite chair. A younger readership can have their news PRINTED OUT without clicking on a site or being barraged from pop-up display advertising.

According to an article in 2018 in the *Washington Post*, in the U.S., weekday print circulation has shrunk from a high of nearly 60 million in 1994 to 35 million for combined print and digital circulation today: 24 years of decline. Advertising revenue has cratered, falling from $65 billion in 2000 to less than $19 billion in 2016. Newsroom employment fell nearly 40% between 1994 and 2014.

According to Statista, there were 1,279 daily newspapers in the United States in 2018. The number of daily newspapers in the U.S. has been on the decline since 1970.

Here's an excellent link to show you how many newspapers were closed, merged or shifted to weeklies:

http://newspaperownership.com/additional-material/closed-merged-newspapers-map/

Impact Locally

Recently, a local weekly newspaper, *The Middletown Press and Journal*, announced it was closing in July 2020 after publishing for 166 years. The newspaper was a critical part of its community and was recognized by the state for its work.

The news of the demise of newspapers gets worse elsewhere as well.

In late October 2020, in a story online at PennLive, the *Philadelphia Inquirer* has announced it will close its print operation facility in Upper Merion Township near Conshohocken in Montgomery County, Pa.

According to PennLive:

> *The newspaper filed a WARN (Worker Adjustment and Retraining Notification) notice dated Oct. 27 with the Pennsylvania Department of Labor & Industry informing the state that the move will lay off 524 people.*
>
> *The newspaper said in the WARN notice that the move comes after a strategic analysis of its print newspaper business and said it would contract with a third-party to print its newspaper.*
>
> *The newspaper said earlier this month that the newspaper would be contracted out to a Cherry Hill, New Jersey printing plant owned by the Gannett Co., which owns USA Today and several midstate papers including* The Evening Sun *in Hanover, the* Lebanon Daily News, *the* Chambersburg Public Opinion, *the* Central Penn Business Journal, The Record Herald *in Waynesboro and the* York Daily Record.
>
> *The* Inquirer *said it informed its employees on Oct. 9 that the facility would close on Dec. 31.*
>
> *The layoffs are expected to take place between Dec. 31 and Jan. 13, 2021.*
>
> *The plant is located at 800 Schuylkill River Road and prints two newspapers,* The Inquirer *and the* Daily News.

> *The* Inquirer *said it is negotiating with a buyer for the 45-acre River Road property, which includes a 674,000-square-foot manufacturing facility that opened in 1992.*
>
> *As of Oct. 14, the* Inquirer *said it employed 1,073 people, and the layoffs would cut the company's workforce almost in half.*
>
> *The newspapers are owned by the nonprofit Lenfest Institute for Journalism, but it operates as a "public benefit corporation," according to the* Inquirer.

From big cities to small neighborhoods, shutdowns occur at a no-longer alarming rate.

According to a story posted by the Nieman Foundation at Harvard, if you want to read a local newspaper on a Monday morning in the state of Wyoming, well, you are out of luck.

From writer Joshua Benton on July 15, 2020:

> *Wyoming has six "daily" newspapers, but now none of them will actually print a paper seven days a week. It could be the first time a U.S. state will publish no newspapers on Monday mornings ... ever.*
>
> *I hope Wyoming residents who like to start their work weeks with a cup of coffee and the local newspaper aren't too attached to the ritual. Because it'll soon be impossible.*
>
> *The* Casper Star-Tribune *announced yesterday that it would no longer be a true "daily" paper, eliminating its Monday and Tuesday print editions next month.*

> *The* Star-Tribune *will continue publishing online news while offering electronic editions of its print newspaper — the e-edition — seven days a week, said President Michelle Robinson. Print editions will be published Wednesdays through Sundays, with plans for an enhanced Sunday newspaper.*
>
> *The change is a reflection of reader demand, Robinson said, with an increasing percentage of readers, in Wyoming and elsewhere, choosing to consume their news digitally.*
>
> *"This is a shift many news organizations are making as more and more readers already consume their news online," she said in a statement, noting that the* Star-Tribune's *website averages nearly 5 million monthly page views. "With these changes we are going to where our customers are."*
>
> *On its own, that's not unusual, or particularly worthy of note to people outside Wyoming. Lots of daily newspapers, seeking to cut staffing and production costs, have eliminated print days, with Mondays and Saturdays being the most common victims.*
>
> *But the* Star-Tribune's *decision will mean that across the entire state of Wyoming, all 97,914 square miles, there will no longer be a single local newspaper printed on Monday mornings.*

The sad decline continues, and it doesn't have to.

In November 2020, the Poynter Institute announced that Gannet offered buyouts and rid itself of 500-some positions:

According to Poynter:

In October, Gannett offered a round of voluntary buyouts to all its employees. Poynter has learned that roughly 600 people opted in and roughly 500 buyouts were accepted.

Gannett, which owns USA Today and more than 250 daily newsrooms, is the country's largest newspaper owner. It employs about 21,000 people, 5,000 of them journalists.

Poynter obtained a copy of a 15-page PDF listing of the job titles of those selected for buyouts. The buyouts include about 60 editors, 19 photojournalists, seven managing editors, three executive editors and 124 reporters.

In the spring, Gannett laid off journalists around the country after its merger with Gatehouse.

In late summer, the company told financial analysts in an earnings conference call that it planned a net addition of journalists through the second half of the year.

Because of the coronavirus, Gannett, like many other media companies, has had furloughs and pay cuts. It closed two newsrooms in Texas, closed printing presses in Montana and California and moved a newsroom out of its building in Ohio. Gannett also has taken on the printing of newspapers of the locally owned Philadelphia Inquirer and McClatchy's Kansas City Star.

A Gannett spokeswoman declined to confirm how many offers were extended and how many were

> *accepted. It is not clear whether some of the positions will be filled by promotions or new hires.*
>
> *"Gannett's furloughs earlier this year and the recent buyouts undermine our democracy," said Jon Schleuss, president of The NewsGuild — Communications Workers of America. "It's a disgrace that any news company thinks it can cut its way to success."*

What is filling the place of newspapers? Some suggest that social media will continue to replace the printed or online newspaper.

I say, really? In the news feed, Facebook and Twitter both struggle with trying to filter content. And their algorithms simply review content posted by many users and determine your preference for what you read. So if you read only one-sided stories, one-sided posts are all you're going to receive in your news feed.

It's the scourge of the Social Media Age.

I've seen two new e-messenging businesses appear in my email from Berks County, right after the purchase and reorganization of the Eagle.

One of those is *Berks Weekly.* The other is a regional e-blast BizNewsPA by Joel Berg, the former managing editor of *Central Penn Business Journal* and *Lehigh Valley Business Journal.*

Of course, these items aren't the size of the typical newspapers that most of us grew up with. The news is carefully trimmed and only the most critical items are posted. Also, most of the e-blasts just provide bullet points, like a television teleprompter reader, with little in-depth analysis of what is going on. There is little or no editorial page submissions or letters to the editor. None of them have major, in-depth features. Everything is in short bites, much like television.

There is very little advertising.

There is so much to me that makes up a great newspaper. It has to have content, lots of content, to be a legitimate news source. It has to have some long-form journalism, either in terms of enterprise or investigative features. It has to have the unique columnists and local segment reporting that is proprietary to the newspaper. These unique items that can't be garnered anywhere else, free of simple news releases and notifications, are what draws readers and subscribers.

I don't like the extended-headline approach of the blasts. I expect so much more from a news source because of my own history as a newspaper reader and subscriber.

Regarding social media: how do you see the news? Scrolling down through friends' news feeds? Waiting for something to turn up in your news feed?

Granted, I learned a lot about what was happening by posts from my social-media colleagues. I find out about birthday celebrations, deaths, births, special occasions and developing news almost on the spot. But I am at the mercy of the feed algorithms and I still miss a lot of what news is: something I want to find out or need to know.

Often I will see a news item in Facebook when I click on Home that was posted seven or eight days ago. It's embarrassing to have to react to that several days after it was posted. And with literally hundreds of friends, how can you read all the posts?

And we know Facebook's and Twitter's policies dictate that if you want to reach everybody in your friends' list, you really have to pay for it. Social media is solidly "pay to play." Facebook and Twitter aren't going to do that for free.

I do get a lot of frustration by trying to find the "news" on social media. I would rather visit the websites.

Here's an interesting story about the *Patriot-News* website, PennLive:

One week in the summertime, during the annual Elizabethtown, Pennsylvania fair, I coaxed my supervisors to set up a table and hand out copies of the magazines we were publishing, including *Central PA Magazine*, *Now* and *Body and Mind*. Since the booth was set up in the early afternoon through the evening, I also took a lot of copies of the current edition. People were happy to pick up free bags, pens, pads, potato-chip clips, static wipes and many other giveaways along with the newspapers and magazines.

I also set up my laptop and monitor to post the latest from PennLive. It was fun to provide a live feed from the website to a large monitor at the fair. I was able to get tons of feedback from readers and digital subscribers. At this time, there was no PennLive paywall: all the content was posted for free.

The fair attendees had a lot of comments. They enjoyed the free website and were happy they didn't have to pay for the news.

I carefully went through the paper and, of course, found plenty of items that were not posted online. Very few display ads were available in any form on the website. There were many more small items in the print version that were not in the daily online version.

Fortunately, I did not encounter anybody saying that we claimed "everything" was online. Clearly online was a source; but if you wanted all the news, you had to subscribe to the printed version, which was complete. At this time, the online material was still being used primarily to drive print subscribers. And we were drumming up subscriptions for the stand-alone *Central PA Magazine*.

Think about it for a second: about two-thirds of digital subscribers and those looking on websites do so on a smartphone. Technologically, there is no way to successfully deliver ALL the items in the newspaper to a small device, or at least one that is decently readable. Large display ad, legal sales, classified ads and much more can't be brought successfully to an image area that is only as large as an open men's wallet.

There are, of course, phone apps to deliver each page. But us old folks have to take off our glasses to read the small, small type.

That's a problem, a big one for digital-only delivery.

And who wants to read irritatingly tiny type on a smartphone? Yet that is the way readers prefer to receive their push notifications and news alerts. That's what they want to do by logging into a digital subscription. That's exactly what they prefer.

It makes you wonder how thorough they are as actual newspaper-source readers. Are they only reading headlines? More so, are they being carefully groomed to consider long-form journalism completely unnecessary?

Probably. Or I would have to conclude, most definitely.

There are so many extra items the printed newspaper provides that simply aren't available on a 3-inch by 7-inch smart screen. Think about all the small correction boxes that are popular. (They really are, according to readers I knew. They always want to see what we got wrong at the newspaper.) Think about the big, colorful editorial cartoons. Think about the comics. How about obituary photos? Or those celebrating a wedding anniversary or engagement?

There are two different types of readers: those who want the news in alerts and push notifications and that's all they need, and lifestyle readers who want the entire newspaper. It is, after all, printed out, so plenty of printer ink is being saved as a result of digital subscribers.

Maybe the amount of waste generated by printing cartridges to digital delivery can be the subject of yet another newspaper feature. I may have to think about writing that.

Chapter 11
NOT IMMUNE

At one time it seemed the healthiest of the newspapers were the thriving town weeklies. Their formula was solid: stick to local events and news and readership will follow. Make the content specific to the community. Do not use commercial copy or too much newswire. Offer a forum for local opinions. Stay local, local, local!

Thriving local sources of the paper, still around and near where I live, in Hershey, Pa., include the *Hershey Sun*, the *Elizabethtown Advocate*, the *Ephrata Review*, the *Lititz Record-Express* and many home-delivered (via email or truck-delivered) merchandisers. A big shout-out to others close by, including the *South Schuylkill News* (owned by MediaNews Group). There are many others.

Some that have fallen by the wayside include the *Columbia Register*. The latest victim as I was writing this book is the *Middletown Press and Journal*, which closed its offices on July 1, 2020.

In Parting Words, *Middletown Press and Journal* publishers Joe and Louise Sukle note that for more than 166 years, the locally owned newspaper weathered all sorts of catastrophes to stay in print. The *Press and Journal* could not weather the downturn that was sharp and severe as a result of the COVID-19 pandemic.

In their words to readers published on June 24, 2020:

Not so long ago, ads from local merchants and service organizations (our bread and butter) began a steady migration to Facebook and Google. Our classified ads were gobbled up by sites like Craigslist and Letgo. If you don't know already, advertising revenue is how newspapers stay in business. How could a small weekly newspaper like the Press & Journal, with a budget for journalists, bookkeepers, sales staff and delivery people, compete with free advertising offered by the internet giants?

How indeed? When I posted the news to my Facebook colleagues, this is what I wrote:

It seems like we are moving to a sad, depressing time in which we get our news solely from the dope (THC) of search and social media. That is, THC: from Trolls, Hearsay and Chaos....

There were layoffs from the weeklies published by Lancaster Newspapers (the disappearance of sports pages, especially in the *Lititz Record-Express*). There have been many other weekly newspapers that have all been impacted heavily by the coronavirus, which directly affected my own employment at the *Reading Eagle*.

We were used to immunity. I live in the Hershey area which, according to my 96-year-old mother-in-law, did not suffer the effects of worldwide recessions and depressions. In the Great Depression, Hershey Company was growing excessively. (In an economic Depression, chocolate is a mood-altering necessity.) In the latest economic Great Recession, a big employer is the Milton Hershey Penn State Medical Center, which has never been dealt a blow by recession, depression, wars or, up to this point, pandemics.

I can remember some layoffs and cutbacks in local newspapers in the small recession of 1991. I can remember how devastated the local community newspapers were by the Great Recession of 2008-2010.

What I remember most is how short-term and fleeting those challenges were, compared to what has been happening today.

I have been preaching for years, echoing the words of the Sukle family: newspaper ads went the way of the Dodo as a result of Google search, Facebook display, Craigslist and all online advertisers.

But what I saw in the past seems steady and repeatable: the best advertising and promotion remains diverse, a combination of print, digital, radio and TV. You need a diversity of channels to promote your business, not a monoculture.

ESSENTIAL: In economic recovery times, those who can re-create their presence in the community the fastest can retake the markets. That is done by print and a combination of digital, radio and TV. A promotional budget using print and other methods is absolutely essential during an economic recovery.

What separates print advertising from the rest? I can tell you what separates it from search engine advertising, whether it is paid search-engine marketing or search-engine optimization.

ESSENTIAL: Search engine advertising cannot SHOWCASE your products. In other words, many buyers will come to you either physically to your store or online to your website, but you first must provide a showcase of what you have. Search-engine customers know what they are looking for already. It's not likely you can sell them something they have never seen before. How many times have you created a sale, if you are a small business, simply because you could SHOW them ALL you have? And give them an experience when they can see for themselves, and touch, taste or smell, firsthand, the products or services you offer?

Print can do that. Some digital display advertising can do that, but in a limited way.

As for readers, how many new buyers do you have as a result of seeing new items on display in the newspaper? There are many instances of how showcasing your product results in loyal customers.

Just ask some of the still-advertising big department stores, such as Boscov's in the Northeast. How about the restaurants with their menus in print? How about having a message with the menus in print that people save in their kitchen cupboards that they refer to again and again when it comes to ordering by phone, or online and getting take-out?

One thing's for certain: advertising peaks at the start of any economic recovery. Plan for it. Be prepared with a plan for it. It has worked in the past and continues to prove its own worthiness.

In an article last year on the website, 247wallst.com, Douglas A. McIntyre wrote that the newspaper industry "has continued its relentless downward spiral, which started with the advent of the internet and accelerated during the Great Recession. The pace of the decline has not slowed. New research shows that over 2,000 newspapers have closed since 2004, a staggering figure given that the industry was once among the largest employers in America."

According to 247wallst.com:

Penny Abernathy, the Knight Chair in Journalism and Digital Media Economics at the University of North Carolina at Chapel Hill School of Media and Journalism, is widely considered the preeminent authority on the number of newspapers in the United States. That is not an easy task, since the number is in the thousands, and some are so small that their fates are hard to track. She is the author of "The Expanding News Deserts," a term coined to describe areas where there is almost no local news coverage.

Abernathy told 24/7 Wall St. that, "It appears at this stage that we've lost approximately 2,100 papers, all but 70 of which are weeklies, since 2004." The industry implosion has left almost half of the counties in America (1,449) with only one newspaper, which is usually a weekly. As of the most recent count, 171 counties do not have a paper at all.

The number of papers in America is currently about 7,000, but as revenue at most of them declines, that number is bound to shrink further. Some newspapers already are close to shuttering. Publishers, both individual owners and chains, have resorted to the equivalent of life support. A recent example is that the Pittsburgh Post-Gazette, which was started 233 years ago, will cut the number of days it is printed from five to three. Two years ago, the paper appeared seven times a week. Management says that it plans to phase out the print edition completely. While the paper may survive online, the "downsizing" will cost dozens of jobs. A drop in the numbers of days a paper appears is part of the industry's playbook to cut expenses.

That is a recurring theme for newspaper owners: the playbook involves cutting expenses and eliminating jobs. It happens over and over and over again.

It's been that way for at least five years. Even in this article on the Medium website from May 2016, the Knight Foundation noted:

Since 2011, the rate of adult U.S. smartphone ownership has increased notably from 46 to 82 percent, and is nearing a saturation point among some age groups. In just the past two years, individual mobile news consumption has grown rapidly. In fact, 89 percent of the U.S. mobile population (144 million users) now access news and information via mobile devices. As news organizations seek to better manage this digital transformation across platforms, engage with their audience and stay competitive, what should they understand about their audience's changing behavior on mobile news? And, how are diverse audiences approaching access to mobile news and information differently?

The reality is: long-form journalism is in jeopardy, badly.

And since the advent of former President Trump's insistence that there is a lot of "fake" news, what other views are the news readers believing?

I remember a conversation with a friend of mine, not employed in the newspaper industry, way back in 1983. This individual sincerely believed that publishing, especially newspapers, was simply a racket: an easy way to make money off the backs of advertisers and subscribers. He believed there was nothing legitimate or noble about what journalists and advertising specialists did. That newspaper publishing was just a scam that has gone on a long time.

I had to remind him that how was he going to find out what was going on locally and nationally from the comfort of a reading chair? About the obituaries and who has passed away with directions about memorial services and funerals? About tracking business information, stock market reports, sports scores or what was on TV? About what jobs were available? Where was he going to get that information in one place?

He turned and walked away. (I could not elicit a "you were right, my friend" from him no matter how hard I tried.)

Return on Investment

Google, Bing and Facebook grab almost all the monies that were originally earmarked, decades before they appeared, for newspapers throughout the world. These days, Google generates about $162 billion in sales.

How many U.S. newspapers would benefit from that?

According to an article in early March 2020, right before the COVID-19 lockdowns and pandemic recession hit, in Statista.com, there were still many newspapers alive and kicking in the U.S.:

> *According to the most recently available data, there were 1,279 daily newspapers in the United States in 2018. The number of daily newspapers in the U.S. has been on the decline since 1970, when there were 1,748 daily news publications in the country. However, given the ongoing struggle of print media around the world, a decrease of around 460 newspapers over several decades is more positive than many might expect.*

A recent report from Journalism.org provides these numbers:

For digital advertising, the numbers are not that fantastic, despite hope that newspaper owners and executives may have:

> *Digital advertising accounted for 35% of newspaper advertising revenue in 2018, based on this analysis of publicly traded newspaper companies. The portion*

stood at 31% in 2017 — but at 17% in 2011, the first year it was possible to perform this analysis.

If you look at a common aggregate, community newspapers with more than 30,000 circulation, for the amount spent on Google search, this is how many newspapers could make ends meet. In the example of the *Reading Eagle*, in numbers reported in the newspaper after the bankruptcy, a "healthy" amount of advertising income is about $21 million a year. That would be sustainable for a mid-circulation (more than 30,000 daily) newspaper.

According to the numbers, that would be 7,714 such newspapers that could be fully funded each year. That number grows substantially for those with less than 30,000 circulation.

The U.S. has only about 1,279 newspapers. With all the Google money, there's room for more than 6,000 additional newspapers in the country alone!

Why do people choose to use Google advertising? To their credit, Google uses some fantastic technology to check click-throughs and engagements that result in sales. So they can provide a more clarified, certain response to online advertising and they analyze what works and what doesn't, taking into consideration terms such as key performance indicators (KPIs) and tracking input into information forms and eventual sales.

Website search-engine companies can provide return-on-investment numbers that excite online advertising enthusiasts and media buyers. They can track a click to a sale, or at least potentially very good leads that can result in a sale. Google, Bing and Facebook are very good at this.

But what is missing? Why are the search-engine sites and social media worried about that approach? What worries media buyers?

I spoke to a LOT of media buyers when I worked as an advertising representative for On-Line Publishers Inc. and the *Patriot-News.*

I spent hours listening to what has worked for media buyer and what hasn't. The best advertisers who had the most success promoting their products recognized the need for a social media presence and to try digital advertising behavior targeting. But even they believed digital strategies were completely inadequate in one area. What was that?

Providing a showcase.

What does that mean?

Just think for a moment about what a search-engine result gives you: a short description of the site and then a link to it. That's it! Usually the result provides no photos or other graphics. There is only a two-sentence-or-less paragraph description with very, very little detail. Then you click to a site and what do you get? It's either a separate landing page or the home page of the website. From there, it is up to the website design or special offers — including dealing with annoying pop-up boxes — to secure a sale or other engagement.

How much do you know about the company that you arrive at via the search link? Do you know what specials are on or do you even have good, high-quality printouts about the items or services they sell? Can you do this without performing extra work by clicking through tabs or using some kind of a toolbar to determine what, exactly, the company is all about, including the makeup of its brand, its history and what kind of experience it wants to provide you, a potential first-time (or in many cases, only-time) visitor?

How about social media sites? Sometimes you get very little description of a branding effort and little in the way that gives you information, most times, of what you are looking for. You are at the mercy of the social-media updates, however consistent and timely or, in many cases, sporadic those updates are. How much are you willing to invest in a purchase in a company or organization if the last update was six months ago?

There may be videos, but in our time-starved culture, where so many individual sites vow for our attention, will that really help you secure a buy?

And what about products that are not advertised on the website or social media site? Sure, sometimes there are special landing pages that resemble a full-page newspaper advertisement. But not very much. And just think of the time spent jumping from the carefully return on investment (ROI)-recorded search link to the page. How about the time it takes to jump from the landing page to the actual website, especially if the link is unclear in the page?

So what does print provide that search links and social media pages can't?

They provide a showcase. You can show in living color what you are selling. You have room, often in a half or full page of a broadsheet print advertisement, to give detail about special products and sales. You can see a coupon or discount offering that can be simply either ripped or cut out. The address and number are big. Often there is a map for the store location. A QR code can also be loaded for a lot more additional information.

But the advertiser can showcase what the company is all about: advertising the brand message; providing a history of the store or service; putting in one or two testimonials from satisfied customers; listing detail about what is on sale and why; and giving the reader a bright, big, beautiful photo of the product or service.

You can brand the ad for take action or simply to promote a marketing message. If done consistently, the brand will remain top-of-mind for readers and buyers.

Even better, it is an opportunity to educate and to provide a glimpse at products or services that readers never were aware of and come across, in discovery, for the first time. Those first-time experiences can easily result in sales.

If you read advertising sales guru Jeffrey Gitomer, you can learn one thing: people often don't realize where they have seen an ad for an item, he notes in one of his sales books (I think it was the "Little Red Book of Selling.") They could have seen it in one newspaper or another, and remember the actual location inaccurately, but it doesn't matter: the ads worked because the reader can remember it, in whatever newspaper it appeared.

For those obsessed with advertising return on investment, or ROI, have to remember that advertising is not ALWAYS about ROI and making a sale. Sometimes it is simply about education. Sometimes it is defining your brand (just ask Gitomer about how important THIS is). Sometimes it is just a wave of the hand: we are here, you should get to know us. Many times it is about showing what kind of merchandise an advertiser has and ways in which they can transform your lifestyle. These ads serve as a way for buyers to keep you, as an advertiser, "top of mind." When consumers think of what they need at certain times in their life, they will think of you, because they see that print newspaper beneath the vase on the kitchen table or on the steps leading upstairs, or wherever in the house the newspaper lands.

Chapter 12
THE LAST STAND

I can remember clearly the day it happened: the *Reading Eagle* bankruptcy in the spring of 2019.

There was a mandatory meeting of all personnel in the company assembly room. We had no advance knowledge of what company executives were going to tell us, nor were we prepared for the news we received.

But company owner and CEO Peter Barbey made the announcement. It was increasingly more difficult to stay financially viable, even during the economic recovery. The company had no choice but to declare Chapter 11 bankruptcy, Barbey said.

There was an article (one of many that carefully, fully and transparently explained what became of the Reading Eagle Company's financial troubles) in the *Reading Eagle*:

> *In general, to declare bankruptcy means the amount of one's debts is more than its assets and income can support, and there are no immediate prospects of paying those debts off in a timely manner.*
>
> *A Chapter 11 bankruptcy — meaning it is filed under Chapter 11 of the U.S. Bankruptcy Code — is often referred to as a "reorganization" bankruptcy and is*

used by a business to reorganize its debt under the protection of the bankruptcy court.

That means the court decides, based upon the assets available at the time, what debtors will get paid. Usually compensation is ensured for workers. At the time, Barbey was spending, each month, about $250,000 of his own money at the time to continue printing the newspaper until bankruptcy was processed and a new buyer was found.

I was astounded: $250,000 per month? That was tough to comprehend. To a multibillionaire, economies of scale indicate that is hardly anything. It would take a long time to spend a billion dollars at $250,000 per month.

But it was easy to see how the company got there.

As I explained in a previous chapter, inexplicably, with no projected and planned path to revenue, the company decided to invest about $37 million in a new Berliner press and custom press building. The plan: attract outside printing jobs. This was in 2009, the beginning of an era in which the tried-and-true newspaper industry was being heavily challenged by a Great Recession and digital search ads. I suppose they thought if it would be built, income would come. They thought wrongly.

But the decision to take on debt to pay for the press and building was a financial albatross. It placed the Reading Eagle Company in heavy debt. So much so that the company defaulted on a loan from a major bank to the tune of $25 million.

Despite some progress on income vs. debt, there was no way the new press was going to pay for itself, let alone be a profitable income-generator for the company.

On May 17, 2019, it was announced on the Eagle website and in the newspaper that MediaNews Group, part of the Alden Hedge Fund and a nationwide media company, had "made the sole qualified bid for Reading Eagle Company's assets.

"In a statement to employees this afternoon, company President and CEO Peter D. Barbey, said: 'We have received two bids to purchase Reading Eagle Company's assets. One of the bids is unqualified. The other bid is.'"

Some former executives tried to interest local businesses in bidding for the newspaper, to no avail.

The bid amount — the ONLY bid amount for the 151-year-old family-owned newspaper, one of the last in the country — announced on May 24, 2019, was a paltry $5 million. It had to be the media steal of the century.

In mid-May, before the sale, the company laid off dozens of workers.

On June 21, MediaNews Group extended employment offers to half the employees of the company, 125 at the time, and 111 accepted.

But more layoffs ensued, in which 19 Reading Eagle employees were laid off in April 2020. This layoff was blamed on the COVID-19 crisis.

Near Philadelphia, MediaNews Group, part of the Alden Hedge Fund, owns the *Reading Eagle*, the *Pottstown Mercury*, the *West Chester Daily Local*, *Delaware County*

Times, *Norristown Herald* and others, including a host of weeklies in the same region.

In the meantime, there has been a sea-change brought about by tough times in advertising (caused by the fact that the dailies refuse to accept a special-sections model). Where once the papers were completely dependent on print and digital advertising to function and pay their staffs, now the focus is primarily on getting digital subscriptions.

Digital subscriptions will pay for editorial staff. More reliance will be on securing subscribers, especially online, than ever before.

Since they don't have a special-sections-first strategy, the surviving daily newspapers have to rely on the model of digital subscribers. Print ad sales for a general newspaper are becoming very difficult to sell. Apparently, the media companies are expecting to continue paying their writers through digital subscribers, NOT ad sales.

Family-Owned

But what went wrong with the family-owned newspapers such as the *Reading Eagle*?

I think they were focused on the logistics of getting a newspaper, any paper, with any content, out there. Deadlines superseded any thoughts of how newspapers could be completely unique. Most "breaking news" was anything but: those with access to news website push notifications and alerts didn't need the old and outdated print form.

In better years, how the *Reading Eagle* succeeded was a focus on the outcomes of municipal meetings, school board decisions, commission reports, hyperlocal events, serving a large amount of community news and upcoming events through the Billboard, a calendar of items. Special projects (including a widely successful favorite pet calendar) and community partnerships with company and non-company events and other things worked well to grow the paper.

ESSENTIAL: But only when the newspaper print content was the most engaging LOCALLY — when it focused entirely on the county of Berks that the Reading Eagle ***served — was financial success possible. Some newspaper special sections were robust. That formula carried for years.***

With no large debt load for newspapers, the formula for local content is successful and sustaining. But if the paper would lapse into canned or wire content, the struggles to attract ad dollars and readers was palpable.

Engaging Audiences

Melody Kramer leads audience growth and development for the Wikimedia Foundation and frequently works with journalism organizations on projects related to audience development, engagement, and analytics. According to poynter.org, Kramer "has spent the majority of her career in public media, where she directed, produced, edited, and wrote material for several shows, including 'Wait Wait Don't Tell Me' and 'Fresh Air with Terry Gross,' and later served as a digital strategist at NPR, where she launched and directed projects that helped NPR build and engage audiences on and off-air."

In a June 2015 article on poynter.org, Kramer wrote about collecting responses from a pool of her newsletter audience about why local news matters. The responses ranged from the police work that local journalism does on reporting what happens with council activities and local government to how in-depth reporting is crucial to help aid and grow a community.

Here is a sampling of Kramer's article:

It's summer now so it's time for a long, juicy beach read on why local news matters.

I posed the question a month ago to my newsletter audience and was expecting four or five responses. I received dozens on why their local newspapers and public radio stations mattered.

I've collected their answers, which I also sent out in my newsletter on June 2, below. If you work in a local newsroom and need a pick-me-up today, I highly recommend perusing the answers. It would also be an interesting question to ask your own audiences. We talk about the importance of local at journalism conferences — and with each other — but our audience also has very good ideas and articulate why they do (or don't) rely on their local news.

Keep in mind, most of these people who answered the questions below live outside of major markets and don't work in news. I've condensed some of their answers for clarity. I would also love to hear your own thoughts in the comments section below.

Local stations are not just about the weather and the road conditions. Those are helpful things to know, but they are not the real heart of what local stations provide. They provide the color of the areas around you; things you might not notice otherwise, but which may be important for your daily life.

For me, being in central Jersey, that means collecting news from "local" stations in NYC and Philly, both of which provide information I care about — about local arts, politics, parks, etc. Now, I know that most of the time I don't hear things about Princeton, where I live, but I do get to hear about regional issues that may have some sort of bearing on my daily life, and that matters. Local reporters are able to pick up on local color and read into situations in a way that national correspondents can't necessarily match.

National correspondents swoop in and provide two minutes of a story, whereas local reporters can revisit a story multiple times to make sure that we, the listeners, fully understand it and its impact on us, if there is one.

The purpose of the local paper or station is to see, know, care about and understand your community in ways your neighbors don't and then share what you find. It's to be perpetual tourist in your town with a side helping of too much empathy.

Check out Wyoming Public Radio: Who else is covering the Wind River Reservation community? Local newspapers, and other community-supported media.

The Current, KCRW, KEXP, and other music-focused public radio stations cover local music scenes in their respective areas as well as lifting up artists that wouldn't get airtime on commercial stations

WAMU and WPFW cover the arts scenes here in DC as well as social justice issues like police violence and District statehood. Who else is doing that?

WHUT screens locally produced cinema and recently engaged in a two hour discussion of race and police violence called Cities in Crisis. None of the local commercial television stations are covering these issues with this depth. On election night, the local news couldn't even get straight what side of town the candidate's respective parties were happening. (Pro tip: Howard Theater is not in Northeast DC.) As I type this, WJLA, Washington's ABC affiliate, has an abundance of crime and tragedy stories on its homepage

Local public media are like public libraries and local museums in that they preserve culture, educate and engage in order to build understanding on important issues that are expensive or difficult to cover. They can also empower people to stand up for justice where there is none.

"For me, the local Washington Post news is critical to my life and public discourse."

I live in DC. I don't care for the hill. For me, the local Washington Post *news is critical to my life and public discourse. That said, the old model of monopoly ad prices supporting big news is gone. We have to find new models to make it work — both in revenue and in reporting.*

Local TV? It's a graveyard of vapid hype.

I live in Brooklyn, and I listen religiously to WNYC. I do get some local Brooklyn based email newsletters, which I've also been trying to pay more attention to.

When I'm looking for local news (as opposed to passively consuming it), I often am in a particular "role" in my head: i.e. I'm looking for events for kids in the neighborhood (mom hat), or I'm wondering about running groups or healthy restaurants (health hat), or someplace to co-work (office hat). I rarely use one source for all of those things, but usually they are local (if not traditional "news") resources.

I wish I could get more worked up about local politics, because in theory I think that's where a lot of change could occur, but it's SO in the details that it's hard to follow unless you can devote a lot of time. I see a big role for local stations in making that relevant and accessible for people — but I wouldn't say that's what they do now

National won't hold your city councilmembers accountable.

In some ways, it would be way easier to simply have every NPR station (for example) run the same, standard schedule, with no local programming. It would truly then be National Public Radio, even if NPR doesn't stand for anything anymore. But, we'd lose an incredible amount if we didn't have local stations. A national station isn't going to break in and tell you about a natural disaster that could wreak havoc. It won't hold your city councilmembers accountable. It won't do deep dives into your local school districts, or talk to interesting people in your area. It'll instead focus on vague things that vaguely apply to everyone, with the majority centered around happenings in New York, D.C. and Los Angeles, simply because that's where the hive mind exists.

But potentially the most tragic thing about not having a local station is losing that connection to your community. Maybe you miss out hearing about speakers coming to town, or local authors who have books coming out, or debates between people wanting your vote. Why would we ever give that up?

Local helps communities get to know each other better

Local radio and newspapers are huge! Public media ties a community together and offers an outlet to share the stories of your neighbors — not only can you gather and send information that relates directly to the community, but you can also get to know each other better.

Reader engagement is absolutely essential. When readers see the value of a newspaper to their daily living, they will stick to it. If newspapers can capture and hold that value, they can survive. But they have to be engaging to everyone, including and especially the businesses that will support them.

When the bankruptcy for the *Reading Eagle* was complete and the sale was made to MediaNews Group, the only regret I have is, one day while sitting in the employee break room, Peter Barbey appeared. I was busy eating lunch, but I turned to him and said hello. In a subsequent email, I thanked him for the opportunity to have the joy of working for the *Eagle*. But before that email, I had a chance to talk to him and ask him, considering his vast wealth, if selling the newspaper really was a good idea. I didn't do it and probably should have, simply to get some closure.

I wanted to ask Peter why he couldn't just make some hard decisions, instituting some painful but necessary changes and reductions to keep the newspaper going. After all, with even an even-$1 billion in my pocket, at a cost of $250,000 per month, I could keep the newspaper going for 333 years.

Without knowing the detail as to why he couldn't sustain the newspaper, without ever asking him, we won't know the answers. That has been difficult for all of us who worked there to wrap our heads around: with so much money, why wouldn't you keep the newspaper printed, considering it was in your family for 151 years?

Reader Loyalty

What creates reader engagement and loyalty? How can you measure it? What works and what doesn't for newspapers?

What do they really want to read about?

In an article in Reuters Institute/University of Oxford, the facts are simple: how much do the stories impact their lives:

People choose to read news that is most relevant to their own lives, and the lives of their families, colleagues and communities, according to new research.

The report by Kim Christian Schrøder, professor of communication at Roskilde University, Denmark, attempts to shed light on the decisions behind readers' preferences as they encounter an increasing amount of content on and offline in a media environment saturated with choice.

The research finds that while digital media provide an immense amount of data about audience news preferences, these tell us little about why readers make the choices they do.

Through interviews with 24 participants, and unique exercises to examine their preferences, the research concludes the key factor in determining news preferences is relevance to readers' daily lives. As one participant put it:

"Something that affects you and your life. That's what you read, isn't it? That's why you inform yourself — because you want to know what's going on and how it's going to impact on you and your life and your job. That's what's important."

Another participant said she chose to read a story because it would be of interest to her son: "That's about the Ford Mustang, so we'd have something to bond over." The report considers this sociable aspect of news as translating into shareability through social media, with news users selecting and sharing stories of interest to their friends and family.

The report also finds:

- *Readers derive their own meaning from stories. A given story may be categorized by one reader as "international," by another as "technology," and another as 'financial'*
- *News today is a cross-media phenomenon, and people often sufficiently informed about major ongoing stories without clicking on every headline*
- *Stories which appear trivial are often valued by readers for their civic implications*
- *There is a natural interest in local news regardless of the topic*
- *The research finds readers can be grouped into four distinct clusters based on patterns of news preferences which all include a diverse diet of news across multiple subjects:*
    1. *People with political and civic interest in news*
    2. *People with a social-humanitarian interest in news*
    3. *People with a cultural interest in news*
    4. *People who seek (political) depth stories*

Report author, Kim Christian Schrøder, a former Senior Visiting Research Fellow at the Reuters Institute for the Study of Journalism, said: "Our research calls for a greater understanding in the media of the complexities of what really drives audience tastes and preferences... journalists should look beyond 'Most Read' lists as a gauge of what news readers really want, and trust their instincts to prioritize news stories with civic value."

What do readers want in a newspaper? There's a simple word: hyperlocal stories. That includes municipal official reports, school board news, events in the communities: in other words, what is going on in everybody's community backyards?

But delving deeper, and based on my own experience, there's more to it. It involves engagement. It involves posting stories of youth involvement in schools and organizations such as FFA, 4-H and other clubs. All youth sports are in this category. The more involved in the news people believe they are, the more relevant their thoughts and opinions are addressed, the more issues that are tackled, the more interest they have in being faithful subscribers.

In *Lancaster Farming*, the weekly farm newspaper I edited, what drove subscriptions were reports on youth in various capacities, including fairs and school events. Who won what contest? How did my child place in whatever event they participated in?

Why should newspapers adapt this model?

One reason only: separation. Standing out from other news organizations. They do so by giving readers something unique, something proprietary and stories gathered in a community where no other news organization dared (or cared) to tread.

The key to newspaper success: give readers what they cannot get anywhere else. That includes specific hyperlocal content that no organization can give. If you provide that, in abundance, then a newspaper will have a loyal group of subscribers.

For the advertising should follow: IF you work on ways to get THEM involved in the news as well.

I discuss that in the later chapter.

Perhaps that's why you read this book, and come to understand the key to the success of a community newspaper.

Toward the end of the book, I will provide a shining example of a successful Pennsylvania newspaper using the formulas I spell out.

Chapter 13
THE LOCKDOWN
(WHEN I BECAME "NONESSENTIAL")

The COVID-19 lockdown in mid-March 2020 dealt a major blow to an already-struggling newspaper industry.

Fortunately, the *Reading Eagle* policy — along with most newspapers — was to provide news about the coronavirus and its impact on the community in front of the paywall, free of charge.

But for a special sections editor? A person who directly or indirectly contributes to a newspaper's bottom line?

Well, I was deemed "nonessential."

(If a person is nonessential, then, I suppose, why is he or she working at all?)

Was the sudden and terrifying work recession as a result of the coronavirus lockdown something of the present-day or was this going to point out something about the business that had been brewing for years?

Was this a sign of the times or a long-standing conclusion to declining print ad revenue?

Here's an article from the April 3, 2020 *New York Times*:

During the Great Recession, more than $60.5 billion in global ad spending evaporated, according to the WARC research group. It took eight years for the industry to fully recover.

Close observers of how the advertising business has fared in recent weeks say the new crisis may be worse.

"It was a seismic shock, possibly the biggest we have faced, ever," said Harris Diamond, the chief executive of the advertising company McCann Worldgroup. "It all took place in a very short period of time, and is having an impact everywhere we communicate."

Overall spending on digital ads for March and April is down 38 percent from what companies had expected to lay out, and ad spending has fallen 41 percent on TV, 45 percent on radio, 43 percent in print publications, and 51 percent on billboards and other outdoor platforms, according to the trade group IAB.

According to *Forbes* magazine in an article on June 2:

The full impact of the COVID-19 pandemic was felt in April. The monthly unemployment rate as measured by Bureau of Labor Statistics reached 14.7% as the U.S. economy lost a record 20.5 million jobs. As businesses shut down, a large majority of Americans were under statewide quarantine laws. With the economy coming to a grinding halt, the advertising and media industries bottomed out. According to the Standard Media Index (SMI), in

April, the year-over-year total ad marketplace dropped by a staggering 35%.

I became a victim of the COVID-19 lockdown and subsequent very slow reopening in early summer. I was laid off from the Reading Eagle, along with 18 others, on April 9, 2020.

I have spent time writing this book, as a result of being unemployed. I have sent out dozens of resumes and cover letters.

Here's one email response to a job posting that I applied for, killed by COVID-19:

Received June 21, 2020:

Dear Andrew,

Thank you for taking the time to submit your application for the position of Director, Publications (job number 494749) with Drexel University.

After careful consideration, we regret that due to COVID-19 we will no longer moving forward with this role.

Thank you for your time and we will be in touch if the role opens back up.

Kind Regards,

Human Resources
Drexel University

ESSENTIAL: Nobody was prepared for the pandemic lockdown. COVID-19 was devastating to a wide swath of

businesses. Newspapers rely far too heavily on restaurant and retail advertising. But if they are careful and consistent, publishing news that has local appeal and engages those businesses and organizations that support it, newspapers can survive. But if newspaper editors and managers slip into worrying too much about production and deadlines and ignoring the keys to sustaining readers, the pandemic just may destroy them. Only time will prove what works.

How can newspapers thrive? The editorial staff must remain committed to hyperlocal coverage. More importantly, special sections are key to survival: creating unique markets that businesses feel a part of and can participate in. And special projects, including, for example, a popular favorite-pet calendar and community partnerships with different organizations, can serve a wide swath of loyal readers.

ESSENTIAL: But only when the content is the most engaging LOCALLY — when writers focus entirely on the county the newspaper serves — is there any hope of financial success. But a focus must remain on special sections and engagement of developing local businesses. A hyper-local mission, engaging local businesses, can sustain any newspaper.

To succeed, local newspapers must follow this formula of local, directed, unique content. But if the paper lapses into carrying mostly canned or wire content, easily obtained for free on the internet, with little or no emphasis on special sections, the struggles to attract ad dollars and readers will become palpable.

Americans still trust their newspapers. Here is a story from the Pew Research Center from April 2020:

Many U.S. news organizations are covering the coronavirus pandemic while themselves facing financial pressure from it. A growing number have announced layoffs, furloughs and other cost-cutting measures as the virus inflicts widespread pain on the economy, and these cuts come on top of years of earlier reductions in newsroom staffing, especially at newspapers.

Amid the financial challenges facing newsrooms, 54% of U.S. adults say the news media have done an excellent or good job responding to the coronavirus outbreak, according to a survey conducted March 19-24 as part of Pew Research Center's Election News Pathways project. A slightly smaller share (46%) says the media's response has been only fair or poor.

Americans rate the news media's response to the virus more positively than that of President Donald Trump, but more negatively than the responses of other key actors, including public health officials, state and local elected officials and ordinary people in their communities.

The public's assessment of this media response comes at a time when most Americans are paying close attention to coronavirus news. Around six-in-ten U.S. adults (57%) say they are following the news about the virus very closely, and an additional 35% are following it fairly closely, according to the survey of

11,537 adults who are members of the Center's American Trends Panel.

In 2020, I was into my third year as Special Sections editor of the *Reading Eagle*, in charge of the Sunday *Homes* and *Drive* (auto) sections in addition to special sections focusing on senior care and retirement (the *50 Plus* section), health care (the *Health & Wellness* section) and others, including *Home & Garden, Bridal Showcase* and others for the cluster of newspapers, including the *Eagle*, owned by the Exton, Pennsylvania-based Philadelphia cluster of the MediaNewsGroup.

On March 18, 2020, I was informed that I needed to pack up my laptop, monitor and other office files and equipment on mandated orders from the governor of Pennsylvania for residents and workers to quarantine at home. At the time, I was commuting as usual from my home in Hershey, Pennsylvania to the *Reading Eagle* offices in Reading, Pennsylvania, a distance of about 57, or about an hour-long round-trip commute.

I remember gathering my things. I was walking out the offices carrying my large monitor and briefcase full of papers when I passed a copy editor, Jerry Reimenschneider, assuring him that I wasn't stealing them, I was going to work from home. (By the way, after my layoff, all equipment was safely returned.) I didn't realize at the time that on that day, a Wednesday, it would be the last time I would step into the *Eagle* offices.

My home office. On March 18, 2020, I was told that I needed to pack up my laptop, monitor and other office files and equipment on mandated orders from the governor of Pennsylvania for residents and workers to quarantine at home.

Working from home poses a distinct challenge for me. I am the kind of guy who needs structure and consistency, and treasures the time I can get away from home in order to work. Work is labor. Home is a place of rest and relaxation. Having an office to go to gives me direction and focus. I am more productive at an office than I am working from home.

But I did so for the next three weeks. It was different but I found myself very productive and focused, thanks to a great home office I keep that has very comfortable furniture and room to work. I stayed in touch with my boss, Dave Mowery. I was content to see this "at-home work lockdown" through.

But I received a call from Mowery and an official from MediaNews Group on Thursday, April 9, which was Holy Thursday and the beginning of Passover. I learned that April 9 would be my last day as a *Reading Eagle* employee.

Of course, there was no ability to have real closure, to say goodbye to my colleagues and trusted friends at the *Eagle*. There was no time to say goodbye to the correspondents or the experienced and talented staff, including the copyreaders and copy chief. As of 5 p.m., that was the end of my tenure at a job I held dearly for five-and-a-half years.

I did have closure through my social media contacts with dozens of correspondents and my network connections. Months right after the layoff I was able to attend what seems like hundreds of Zoom and Skype meetings with my network contacts. But it isn't the same. Zoom meetings are so awkward and inefficient, so stymieing and counterproductive, not to mention simply exhausting. You have to hope your Wi-Fi connection is strong and remains intact and your computer doesn't fry. It is nowhere near the same of meeting in person to read body language and to hear and understand conversation, to truly network.

In subsequent months I sent out more than 126 resumes and cover letters and participated in many virtual job interviews.

Since March 8 of 2020, I have not seen my family, met with them in person. However, I converse with them regularly over the phone. At one time my brother Robert had health issues and I was communications liaison with my family with his condition from entering the hospital until he was safely home. And after six months I have not visited or been with Robert in person.

I remain in constant touch with weekly network groups in Berks County, including Entrepreneurs' Connection, PAK and the Eastern Pennsylvania Business Owners Network. I am in touch via social media with many former correspondents.

But it is not the same. I for one have been DONE with this self-quarantine and lockdown since at least mid-June of 2020. As I write this in mid-November 2020, I desperately want to return to the normalcy of working at an office. I am beginning to wonder if we shall ever return to that form of "normal."

What are my days like since the job layoff and pandemic lockdown? They are full, including writing this book and another book about looking after my mother-in-law, Mary, who suffers from vascular dementia. I also write as a correspondent for the weekly community newspaper, the Hershey Sun and am contributing articles to Delmarva Farmer in Easton, Md. and for Philadelphia Medicine working out of Sinking Spring, Pennsylvania.

I wanted to do this in "semi-retirement" if I could have made it to 70 years old. That's what I was looking forward to do. But it's far too early for me to retire. I long to return to full-time work.

So these are what my days are like. Typically, I am up at 6:30 a.m. and out for a walk with my wife, Debbie, at 7. I'm back for breakfast at 8 a.m. I am in the office answering emails at 9 a.m. At 10 a.m. I am either researching or writing until I have to leave the office, because Debbie works at home and cannot afford any distraction. So I leave to work on my laptop in the kitchen until lunch at noon.

After lunch, I head to the Penn State Milton S. Hershey Medical Center University Fitness Center for an hour strength and conditioning workout in its excellent gym, fully masked at all times. I have NEVER worked out anywhere without full masking, and that includes other gyms in Hershey, since the start of the pandemic. I return home to answer emails using my smartphone about 2 p.m. Then from 2 p.m. until about 5 p.m., I am either researching or writing. After about 6 p.m., I have supper and spend the rest of the early evening working on social media and reading. I rarely watch any television.

I think the "tyranny" of sameness is in place here, as there is very little variation from day to day. Debbie and I are still very worried about the COVID-19 pandemic and do not attend any indoor events. She loves the mask. I of course hate it. We have eaten out once, alfresco, at a very decent local restaurant. It is tiring to mask-up everywhere, especially when we go to get groceries.

Other than maintaining my large vegetable garden, there is very little joy in my work life now, but the writing fills the time nicely. Actually, I really prefer to read and review books; but that is a book I will write another day.

Dr. Ryan Howes, writing in Self.com recently, had this to say about finding joy during the pandemic:

Even with growing numbers of sick people and death tallies skyrocketing, a portion of our society is, honestly, feeling okay during this pandemic. Or even more than okay. (Some of the time, anyway.) In my practice as a clinical psychologist, I'm mostly hearing about anxiety related to illness and the economy. But some of my clients have expressed giddiness — not about the many abysmal parts of this pandemic, of course, but about how they've changed aspects of their own lives in response to it. They even sometimes feel joy.

Even for those of us who are stumbling upon positive feelings right now, the emotions I'm talking about aren't really manifesting as "I'm so glad this pandemic is ravaging the planet because I love my life right now." It's more: "The abject horror of this pandemic is so clear — how can I be happy with anything in my life when so many people are suffering?" The truth is that, as humans, our emotions are endlessly complex. There's a huge range of "right" ways to feel about all of this.

Fear, anxiety, sadness, grief, anger, and boredom are definitely the most common emotions I'm hearing about at this time. There's so much pain and uncertainty coming across our news feeds that this all makes sense. But I keep hearing about positive emotions to the point that I want to let anyone who's feeling guilty about that know they're not alone. Here's a sample of the less-than-terrible feelings I'm hearing from clients and colleagues:

Belonging: *Those fortunate enough to be sheltering with people they enjoy might be feeling an extra sense of belonging right now. Even if you're not in* *this exact situation, thanks to means of connection like Zoom calls, many people are finding a significant uptick in their social bonds even at a time of widespread social distancing. Some of my clients who have dealt with anxiety, depression, or chronic illness for years also report feeling more understood and included because nearly everyone is wrestling with some of the same challenges that can come from these conditions.*

Comfort: *Along with the inundation of negative news, there is also an outpouring of words of encouragement and kind gestures. Some of my clients are loving how so many friends and loved ones are reaching out and how celebrities are offering messages of hope. Many clients are also feeling deep gratitude for the health care workers and people in various service industries who are taking risks on their behalf.*

Excitement: *If you're into politics, statistics, epidemiology, or disaster movies, you might feel an unexpected sense of excitement (and extra guilt about it). There's so much happening on a historic level, with so much to learn and critique. If the new coronavirus hasn't impacted you or anyone you know in a serious way, it might feel like all of this is happening from enough of an emotional distance that you can watch it unfold like some kind of surreal movie.*

Joy: *Being stuck at home can be heaven for the introverted crafters, home gardeners, tinkerers, and* *jigsaw puzzle enthusiasts who normally have to interact with others more than they'd like. If you thrive in a small world where you can focus on solitary hobbies, having an excuse to spend so much time at home can be your happy place.*

Relief: *One of my clients said these times remind her of showing up at school to find a substitute teacher is taking over what's normally a rigorous class: You probably feel relieved because the expectations are lower and there's less to do. This new coronavirus-induced relaxing of social rules gives some people permission to do things they found challenging before, like turning down plans, asking for help without worrying about seeming needy, and setting boundaries. It can feel like it's easier to get a pass for some things than before.*

So, yes, for some people, there are some potential bright spots in a dark and dismal time. But feeling even a little bit positive in the midst of so much awfulness can also make you feel just as much guilt.

It's okay to feel some moments of happiness right now. It doesn't make you a monster. Actually, it can be really helpful. The new coronavirus pandemic unfortunately isn't going anywhere anytime soon. We all have to figure out how to get through this in a way that's emotionally sustainable over the long run. Finding moments of joy where you can might help you endure.

There's also the fact that, even if you have to dig deep, you'll probably notice that you don't only feel okay (or even happy) right now. Having a lot of conflicting feelings is part of being human.

"We all have different parts [of ourselves] that feel different things and will polarize around times of crisis," Richard C. Schwartz, Ph.D., a psychologist and founder of Internal Family Systems, tells SELF. Internal Family Systems is a therapy approach that looks at various "parts" of a person and their relationships with each other. Think of the Pixar movie Inside Out, in which all of the emotions are different characters, then add a few like your critical voice, your inner child, and your rebellious side.

As it turns out, Schwartz is also experiencing a range of emotions due to this pandemic. "Parts of me are thrilled to be off the road and able to rest and catch up and spend time with my wife," he says. "At the same time, other parts are critical of me for feeling happy while so many others are suffering with this.... I have parts that feel I should be doing much more to help people and other parts that say I'm at risk — I turned 70 this year and have a history of asthma — and should never leave the house."

According to Schwartz, it's natural and even healthy to have mixed feelings right now. "Having [multiple] emotions about anything is expected and not something to feel guilty about," he says.

So, instead of beating yourself up about any positive feelings you may have about how your life looks, Schwartz recommends trying to be curious about them. "Listen to each part separately, learn why it's feeling the way it is. If you can do this, what you will hear will make some sense and you can extend acceptance and compassion to [yourself]," Schwartz says. "It just helps to know that it's normal to have parts that have very different experiences."

This kind of self-examination might rustle up some less-than-pleasant emotions if you realize positivity is masking more negative feelings, like fear or grief. While it can be a good thing to try to find upsides to a devastating situation where you can, that's different from focusing on the good as a way of ignoring your other feelings. If you think you're dealing with the latter more than the former, I'm going to gently urge you to try to process the more negative feelings when you think you're ready. Focusing on bright spots as a way of avoiding tougher emotions is a distraction that can make distressing feelings even more overwhelming when you do eventually confront them.

"Rather than try to counter fear with positive feelings, I recommend that you focus on the fear," Schwartz says. "You might be able to see that scared part and hold it in a comforting way. Too many people try to override or ignore their fear by focusing on other emotions like courage or [finding] ways to distract from it. This only makes the fearful part feel abandoned and more scared, and you have to work harder to keep it exiled."

I have a saying I've used with my clients for years: Feelings are nonnegotiable. They aren't right or wrong or good or bad. They just are. Behaviors can be constructive or destructive, but feelings aren't a matter of choice. Whatever you feel at this bizarre time on our planet is fine.

If you're surprised or even ashamed of some of the feelings you're having, follow Schwartz's advice and get inquisitive about the parts of you that feel a certain way, which may help you understand those emotions better and develop compassion for yourself.

And, in the end, remind yourself that you aren't a bad person if part of you is enjoying some aspects of your new life a little (or a lot). You can be rigorous about behaviors like hand washing and disinfecting, but drop the judgment about what you feel. If you can find some joy in this time, consider that a gift, and try to be grateful for it.

Where is my joy in this pandemic, as I am quarantined at home for months on end and have to help my wife care for her mother, who is 96 years old, has trouble hearing and is an advanced stage of vascular dementia?

I have sent more than 126 resumes and about another 70 cover letters out for potential work. I think one of the worst things that can happen to you is losing your job at 59 years old. It could literally be the worst time to lose your job, because age discrimination will inevitably kick in. Age discrimination is real and I highly suspect I have become the victim of it.

But age discrimination can be very difficult to prove. However, I have compiled lots of evidence that my experience in writing and editing means little or nothing during a job search, especially these days.

It used to be that experience and training were everything to securing a job. Now I have come to realize that they have little to do with having a job. Of course, you can meet the basic requirements. In the end, you have to be young, affordable, trainable and, in the end, well-liked. Or so it seems.

What is COVID-19 Joy?

What the pandemic has brought us is a way of looking at how important our lives are apart from a steady job, a commute to an office, working overtime and focusing entirely on our careers. It has forced us to focus on our lives and rediscover what is really essential and what is really critical to our happiness.

Will the world be changed by it? You know what, I don't really think so.

The cliché of the "new normal" will be tossed out in years to come. I think a lot will come back. For those who work at home, what will stop them from double-dipping and working two full-time jobs, illegally? The purpose of having an office is to exact disciplinary measures and to monitor the work behavior of staffs.

How many of us can stand being at home for this length of time, isolated with our small worlds of office and family, especially those of us who are used to a lot of human contact? About those of us who need structure in our work and home lives? About the need to be with people and conduct ourselves in a career that used to have lots of human contact and freedom to move about without wearing a mask and having to maintain six feet of physical distancing?

Everybody at the time of this writing wants the pandemic to end.

What will working for a newspaper entail post-coronavirus?

I can only speculate, but I think many editorial and advertising staff people won't return to an office. Zoom meetings, mostly on a daily basis, will remain for the future. I think those that have endured the pandemic and remained open will stay that way. But for many newspapers, with seemingly dozens of staff members, what will the future entail?

Making calls and doing work from home will remain for many of us, sadly, and probably indefinitely. But somewhere there are journalists who are recently graduated and have worked for some time in a newspaper office. They will miss the camaraderie, dearly. They will miss the focus and structure of an actual office. They will miss their colleagues. They certainly will long for the network and professional contacts they established so carefully post-university, and will long for much of that to return.

Because working from home can get pretty damned tiring.

When those same journalists turn into editors and executives, they will pine for the days when there was an office location, focus and structure, and I think they will bring all that back. I yearn for that day, right along with them.

What do I want to do at the end of this terrible, newspaper-destroying pandemic? I want to hug my family. I want to go, maskless, shopping and to restaurants. I want to travel a lot more and visit all the places that fortunately will be open post-pandemic lockdown. I want to move freely about my community and my country.

I will never, ever take that for granted.

Mostly I want to connect, in real life, with others in my professional network, my colleagues and friends, and let them know how much I have truly missed them.

I will never take the work we did together for granted, ever again.

I have been busier than ever post-lockdown, numbering, as I publish this, nine months. Nine months of complete work disruption. But what I always thought was that I work a lot harder in a layoff than I did when I was working. I try to leave time to take long walks, go to the gym (I always wear a mask) and make some quality time to spend with my lovely wife, Debbie.

Until the day that "normal" is welcomed back like a long-lost, dear friend.

Chapter 14
RE-INVENTION

According to Data USA, there were 14,004 journalism degrees awarded in 2017, growing at a rate of about 1.08% per year.

I was astonished at this number. Despite a field that continues to contract and diminish, graduates still see the rewards and glory of covering the news. The average journalist makes $72,366, growing by a rate of 2.84%

The journalism-degree workforce, which includes editors and writers, ad sales representatives, public-relations officials and marketing professionals, totals 2.27 million. Average employee age is 40.

According to Journalism.org, using data from the Bureau of Labor Statistics' Occupational Employment Statistics, 37,900 people worked as reporters, editors, photographers, or film and video editors in the newspaper industry in 2018. That is down 14% from 2015 and 47% from 2004. Median wages for editors in 2018 were about $49,000, while for reporters, the figure was about $35,000.

It costs a good amount to obtain a degree. According to the website, post-secondary tuition is $6,885 per semester, on average, for in-state students and $30,696 for out-of-state private colleges.

According to CostOwl.com: Chances are good that if you want to become a journalist, it's definitely not for the money. The salary statistics for journalists bear this notion out. According to the Bureau of Labor Statistics (BLS), reporters and correspondents earn a median annual income of $35,870. Using data from the National Association of Colleges and Employers (NACE), the average starting salary for journalism majors comes out at $38,400. Forbes, however, notes that journalists with a graduate degree earn $40,000 (2007 statistics).

From what I have learned from my journalism colleagues, a working journalist makes about $40,000 per year. You won't get rich being a working journalist. The love of the field is all you'll have, or need.

But what's in store for those who want to enter the field?

Average salaries for all reporters, correspondents and broadcast news analysts in 2013, according to Career Trend, was $37,090. According to the website, employment of reporters, correspondents and broadcast news analysts is expected to decline 13% from 2012 to 2022, from data obtained from the Bureau of Labor Statistics.

"This is a sharp decline compared to the average job growth rate, an 11 percent increase for all occupations through 2022," said Career Trend.

Today's average pay for a journalist, according to the website, PayScale, is $40,839.

See what I mean?

If you decide to make a career of it, it means you don't intend on making a lot of money but are passionate about the field. You would be drawn to it simply by a love of the field. Certainly there are few financial rewards.

Along the way, if you are still interested in pursuing a career in journalism, and you have selected newspapers, this is — unfortunately — what you have to be prepared for:

- It is great if you work for a family newspaper. Most likely, if it remains solvent, and the owner is passionate about the product, you can negotiate a higher pay, especially if you move to a general manager position, such as department editor, managing editor or editor-in-chief. In the case of my own career, I was editor of the *Lancaster Farming* weekly and business editor (later special sections editor) at the *Reading Eagle*. There is absolutely no job security.
- If you work for a national chain newspaper, keep in mind that as soon as the economy sours, the organization will make cutbacks in ways even you can't predict. There is no guarantee your position or job are secure. Keep your resume fresh at all times.
- If you can tolerate the unpredictability of this field, and you are open to a variety of challenges and don't mind a layoff every now and then, you can derive some joy when you are employed.
- As a reader, keep in mind, special sections, pages and columns will not last forever. In one year, there were at least a dozen design and content changes to one local newspaper (I've seen it at the *Reading Eagle*.) As

a reader, you can only hope the decisions made are the right ones for you.

What about the future? What will newspapers be like?

Today's decisions obviously affect tomorrow's newspaper readership. Long-form journalism will exist, but these are the trends for the next 10 years:

In March 2014, HuffPost published a review of major front-page newspapers all the way back to 1984. The organization published the covers of significant events from each year. It is amazing. At heart, news was reported in much the same way as the current day. Some formats were tweaked, but the hammers (main headlines), kickers (headlines over the top of the main headlines) and deck summaries (the headlines appearing beneath the main kicker headline) are much the same. The formats show little changes, other than some major ones to the authors (bylines) that showcase either an email contact, Twitter account or some other way of reaching the writer. So many of the successful formats, even going back 40 years, will continue to remain.

In July 2020, *Editor & Publisher* noted that most newspapers are using an email newsletter to feature their news coverage on at least a daily, if not twice-daily basis. I think there will be at least 4 posts per day in 2030.

Digital platforms will exist for all news organizations with a gradual decline in print. The community weeklies and some print will remain, but only for the most diehard of newspaper readers. However, the digital format will not work well for community weeklies, simply because hyperlocal coverage will remain the bread-and-butter of weekly newspapers.

However, more weekly newspapers will be lost. In an article in the March 21, 2018 *Washington Post*:

> *In the U.S., weekday print circulation has shrunk from a high of nearly 60 million in 1994 to 35 million for combined print and digital circulation today — 24 years of decline. Advertising revenue has cratered, falling from $65 billion in 2000 to less than $19 billion in 2016. Newsroom employment fell nearly 40 percent between 1994 and 2014.*

In the June 27, 2020, *New York Times*, opinion columnist Ross Douthat noted:

> *What will this 2030-in-2022 look like? First, certain key cultural institutions will be increasingly consolidated and concentrated, academia and journalism especially. In the newspaper industry, much of this process happened already, but COVID-19 is delivering a swifter* coup de grâce *to midsize daily newspapers and online start-ups, and handing advantages to a few national entities (ahem) that they might have otherwise taken five or 10 more years to gain.*

That means much smaller newspaper staffs and many missed opportunities to report the news. It means shrinking print size and more sharing of resources from sister newspaper companies (we've seen that in the *Reading Eagle*). It means, as it has for the past two decades, very few newspaper startups, if any. I think the newspapers we have today — as I write this, in November 2020 — will be the most we will have, sadly.

What about the far future of newspapers? How about 30 years from now? What will BE the newspaper?

That's as yet to be determined, but for now, please follow this line of educated guesswork from these questions:

Newsrooms have to adapt. But what could possibly take the place of newspapers?

Are newspapers a "perfect medium?"

Author Isaac Asimov thought as much about a "sister" to a newspaper: how about the ordinary book? Make this comparison to digital delivery of the news:

I can't remember the quote in its entirety, but at one time the futurist and science fiction writer, the Good Doctor Isaac Asimov, wrote about what he considered the "perfect medium" for knowledge. Something he can fold up and take with him in his pocket on a subway or train, and something that he could throw across the room and it would contain all its information with little or no damage. That he could command to open up in any place instantly. That could last for a long time and didn't need a battery or a connection and was inexpensive to own.

What was that medium? It was the paperback book.

The same can be applied to newspapers, I think. Already a tried-and-true medium, but changes to how we receive the news will continue to evolve. But nothing beats the print newspaper of today. Nothing.

The bright side: you don't have to print anything out! No batteries required!

What will newspapers be like 30 years from now?

I think the technology will be advanced enough that newspapers will be available via some type of membrane technology that could convey photos and the printed word via a "news cloth" — technology similar to a smartphone but built of some type of polyester-like material that could be folded many times, like a napkin, conveying to us instantly timely, crisp news updates whenever and wherever we want. In 30 years, newsprint will have disappeared, except for a few publishers.

After all, vinyl records are still around and picking up in popularity, aren't they?

Career Reinvention

For the hundreds of displaced print journalists, does the future look bleak?

I really don't think so. A few of my colleagues went into their own businesses. Several others have taken jobs elsewhere and their working situation is quite different. Some of them have moved into entirely different careers in real estate sales, home health services and others.

I think the coronavirus layoffs are going to make a lot of journalists rethink their career goals in a profound and everlasting way. Some have been used to being reporters and editors for so long that they believe they cannot change. They have not experienced a lot outside their newsroom "beat," covering local government, courts, business or schools. But along the way is another story.

Along the way, they came across their "mirror" colleagues in positions such as information officer, marketing director, public relations representative or spokesperson. Those same positions require the same amount of education and experience. Those positions require experience in writing and editing. The dynamics of the work differ, sometimes greatly, from the work in a newsroom. But there is a common ground on reporting the information in a fair, balanced way.

There is always sales. At one time I moved from an editorial career to one in sales. There are so many media-related sales opportunities out there, in television, radio and print. There are also sales positions in many industries.

So the transition to other work is not without its challenges, but is quite possible. It takes work. But work exists in corporate communications and marketing, public relations and promotions in a variety of companies.

Companies will always have stories to tell, and the journalists — what they call communication specialists — will tell them.

According to the U.S. Bureau of Labor Statistics, in 2019, there were about 275,000 employees in public relations-type jobs. Median pay was about $61,000 per year.

Chapter 15
CHANGING REALITIES

Some changes these experts expect to see in the coming months or years might feel unfamiliar or unsettling: Will nations stay closed? Will touch become taboo? What will become of restaurants?

But crisis moments also present opportunity: more sophisticated and flexible use of technology, less polarization, a revived appreciation for the outdoors and life's other simple pleasures.

— Politico

Into the end of 2020, the COVID-19, or coronavirus pandemic, raged on. It was steady through the summer of 2020 but, after the election in November, outbreaks increased dramatically everywhere.

In mid-July that year, outbreaks were spiking after several states reported increasingly confirmed-positive cases of COVID-19. They included Texas, Louisiana, Arizona and Florida.

But the incidences of positive tests and hospitalizations climbed to record-breaking levels by mid-November 2020.

Some again closed their doors to businesses, such as Texas. Some, including hotspots for the pandemic in western Pennsylvania, closed the bars. Restaurant capacities were severely limited. The situation was dire for restaurant and retail businesses.

But that would be short-term, until and unless the virus was stopped in its track or, more likely, a vaccine came to be. As of this book's press time, a vaccine, successfully tested by Pfizer, was awaiting approval by the Food and Drug Administration and Centers for Disease Control and Prevention for emergency use.

According to a story in the July 1, 2020 MSN, BioNTech of Germany and the U.S. pharmaceutical giant Pfizer reported positive preliminary results from a joint project to develop a coronavirus vaccine. Eventually all three phases of testing the mRNA-based vaccine, never used on humans before, created a 95% efficacy rate with no dangers to the public.

From MSN:

Known as BNT162b1, it produces antibody responses at or above the levels seen in any convalescent serum — blood from people who have recovered — at relatively low doses, according to BioNTech CEO Ugur Sahin.

The preliminary data come from a so-called phase 1/2 trial that aimed to show the vaccine is not toxic and triggers an immune system response to prepare the body to fight off the virus.

Of 45 people aged 18 to 55 who took part in the trial, most received two doses, 21 days apart, of the vaccine or a placebo.

A relatively high number of participants developed a fever after the second dose, according to a study uploaded on the pre-publication website medrxiv.org. But this is not unexpected and is not considered a stumbling block.

The vaccine relies on messenger RNA, genetic code that slips into human cells to make them generate antibodies that are specifically tailored to the coronavirus.

Several companies have published results from the initial phases of clinical trials stating that their experimental vaccines cause an immune system response.

A total of 23 COVID-19 vaccine projects have launched clinical trials on humans, says the London School of Hygiene & Tropical Medicine.

Several have moved to phase two or to phase three, when they are injected into thousands of volunteers to evaluate their effectiveness, monitor side effects and collect other information that will allow them to be used safely.

A vaccine created by the U.S. biotech firm Moderna and one from Oxford University in collaboration with British-Swedish firm AstraZeneca are among those which are in the most advanced stages of development, along with several Chinese projects.

These include one from the company CanSinoBIO, which has received permission to administer the vaccine to Chinese soldiers.

But jobs continued to be lost across the U.S.

In a snapshot, the *Washington Post* recently reported that, by early May 2020, 10 million low-wage workers had lost their jobs in just six weeks, more than the entire toll of the Great Recession:

The world is in the grip of the most devastating pandemic in more than a century, and the economy shed a record-demolishing, livelihood-destroying total of 20.5 million jobs in April as the unemployment rate hit its highest levels since the Great Depression.

While the world awaits an effective vaccine, what will happen to newspapers and their staffs?

Already the newspaper model is being co-opted by political groups.

A report in an early October 2020 issue of the *New York Times* spoke about its investigation of a newspaper called the *Maine Business Daily*, "part of a fast-growing network of nearly 1,300 websites that aim to fill a void left by vanishing local newspapers across the country. Yet the network, now in all 50 states, is built not on traditional journalism but on propaganda ordered up by dozens of conservative think tanks, political operatives, corporate executives and public-relations professionals, a *Times* investigation found."

According to the *Times*:

> *The sites appear as ordinary local-news outlets, with names like Des Moines Sun, Ann Arbor Times and Empire State Today. They employ simple layouts and articles about local politics, community happenings and sometimes national issues, much like any local newspaper.*
>
> *But behind the scenes, many of the stories are directed by political groups and corporate P.R. firms to promote a Republican candidate or a company, or to smear their rivals.*

Print Newsrooms

What is work life like for those who are still employed in print newsrooms?

Already some have been assigned permanent workspace at home. Some go to a satellite office half the week to work. Some may not be returning to the standard office at all, resigned to working out of their homes permanently.

My wife, Deb, is one in which she was sent home and, as of this writing, continues to work out of her home office.

My colleagues who were spared layoffs are working from home, participating in weekly Zoom meetings to review their assignments and they email their stories. (Some can log in to the network used to process stories from their home office.) Some have returned to the work office on a very limited basis. Others have no idea if or when they will return to the office, at least when this was written in November 2020.

Some who work in the newspaper industry have been asked to take weekly furloughs to weather the enormous downturn in paid advertising. I know quite a few of those whose jobs were cut, including mine, in early April 2020.

What does this mean for the future of newspapers?

It means that long-form journalism, such as series and exposes, could be in jeopardy. Forced to work with limited contact, unable to efficiently network as they did before the quarantines and work lockdowns, journalists will have to deal with shrinking news resources, including lead generators and network contacts. In lockdown, how can journalists dig up stories? Many stories will be one-contact.

The space for editorial has been shrinking significantly. Paring-down of stories has taken place on a massive scale. The robust sections are cut to the bones. This is very troubling to an industry that has already been significantly scaled back because of ever-shrinking ad revenue, as Google and Facebook gobble up most advertising dollars.

Can a robust newspaper industry exist post-pandemic?

That all depends on the definition of post-pandemic. Few experts know when that will be. I have been saying since the pandemic began it will take a vaccine, and only a vaccine, to bring us back to normal or even remotely near-normal. When will that be? It's the $60 million question.

Or, should I say, $21.43 trillion.

According to the U.S. Bureau of Economic Analysis, current-dollar gross domestic product increased 4.1 percent, or $848.8 billion, in 2019 to a level of $21.43 trillion, compared with an increase of 5.4 percent, or $1,060.8 billion, in 2018.

Wages for journalists will stay low, near an average of $40,000 per year. In some places, that would be considered minimum wage. It is barely above poverty in most regions. In urban areas, it is poverty.

So many former newspaper journalists would have to enter the world of corporate communications, marketing or other types of public relations in order to sustain a career they planned for, studied and graduated from college for years ago.

A longtime colleague of mine, journalist Carol Ann Gregg, had this to say:

> *I was working for Allied News from 1988 to 1990 and left for* Pennsylvania Farmer, *which turned out to be a short-lived opportunity. That was when the magazine publishing business began to shrink. I returned to Allied, our local twice a week paper, in 2005 and was laid off in October 2011. In 2005, there were 12 people on staff. Now there are 3: one advertising, one reporter and one utility person who is there 10 a.m. to 2 p.m. In 1988, the newspaper was owned by Dow Jones. Now it's owned by a holding company that owns dozens of small papers with no ties to the community or the readers. It is a sad state of affairs. I can't afford to even contribute there for what they pay.*

Allied News is in Grove City and covers eastern Mercer County, Pennsylvania. It is a sister paper to *The Sharon Herald.*

Gregg told me the *Herald* just went from 7 days a week to 5 days. Tuesday is now online only and Saturday and Sunday have been merged into a weekend edition that comes out on Saturday. These are "tough times for print media," Gregg said.

There will be some re-invention and examination of new career opportunities.

For those who remain in the industry, if they are happy with sub-par wages, that is their prerogative.

It will depend on newspaper leaders. For those used to the printed word, many will have to adjust to a permanently online world.

Newspapers MUST adopt a special-sections format merely to stay afloat. But they remain spooked by that separation of church and state dogma that they can't get out of their heads. It doesn't have to be that way, or at least to the extent newsrooms make it. That HAS to change, or it's all over.

We can only hope that news organizations can provide the filter, and fact-checking, to ensure the news is reported accurately, even in a digital landscape.

We shall see.

The realities have been stark for journalists. Specialists other than weekend editors are being eliminated. The harsh reality is that the section editors are taking on a lot more responsibilities, extending their time and workload to a degree that may not be sustainable.

And many, many companies are choosing to extend the work-from-home mentality. I have only one question about that: if mobile work is all that is ever done, isn't there a worry that some workers will take on another full- or part-time job and double-dip? What of double-dipping in the age when there is no at-home supervision of work and where employers really have only a vague notion of what employees have been up to? I don't want to suggest a George Orwellian, 1984-like scenario with cameras on workers. But if you think about it, the supervised structure would prevent such fraudulent acts such as double-dipping.

Will journalists come back to an "office" post-pandemic? I really don't think so, for many news organizations. At some point in the near- or far-future, "going to the office" may devolve simply into a quaint, quirky memory. But the camaraderie and think-tank-like mentality of a newsroom will be irretrievably lost.

Chapter 16
NEWSPAPER SUCCESS

With the help of a colleague from my work at the *Patriot-News*, I was able to secure freelance correspondent work with a local weekly newspaper, the *Hershey Sun*.

The *Sun* is published by Deb Buffington. Drew Weidman is editor.

The total full-time staffing for the *Sun* is small. But what makes it work — and successfully, with no interruptions to publishing throughout the COVID-19 crisis — are the many local contributors, including a huge amount of correspondents.

For a time, I was the Derry Township (Hershey is an unincorporated state entity) correspondent. I covered township supervisor and planning commission meetings. I did some features on transportation and long-term municipal planning.

But for all purposes, all content is local, with local columnists covering surrounding municipalities, including township supervisor, planning commission and school boards. Local government reportage is top priority. No local newspaper covers the municipality as well as the *Sun*.

Readership and subscribership is growing. The advertising is robust. There are special pages with a local focus from time to time. And it is a bedsheet format — the widest newspaper I know. There are plenty of local columnist reporting, lots of letters to the editor, commentary from those who understand the town's history, large photo pages highlighting aspects of the municipality that are little known, plenty of items (including photographs) from the historical society, coverage of high school sports . . . the paper is full of nothing but local, local, local, even from adjoining municipalities.

Why is the *Sun* successful?

What makes it so special and robust during these times?

The *Sun* "gets" it. The owners and managers understand the formula for success because they place a heavy emphasis on not only great readership with a cool and user-friendly, clean website but special editorial sections that focus on the business of what they call "Sun Country." They have a hyperlocal focus. They engage both the loyal readers and advertisers.

Here is a formula for newspaper success:

- Hyperlocal coverage. Every week, cover all your municipal and school board meetings and report on them in a timely manner.
- Place copy that is proprietary, written specifically for the coverage area. Define your coverage area carefully and report on it.
- Don't use a lot of newswire material, because readers can get that for free almost anywhere on the web.

- Engage advertising and promote the newspaper through the leadership of special sections.
- Develop special sections, if possible.
- Be out and about in the communities, involved in all community events, including celebrations downtown, parades and even high-school sports. Engage with the community whenever and wherever possible.
- Special promotions. Publish favorite and award-winning pet calendars, recipes, etc.
- Get feedback on a consistent basis from readers and advertisers.

That's it! The golden key is in the hands of community newspapers to weather the effects of recessions and pandemics.

Long live the *Hershey Sun*!

Chapter 17
THE SCRAPBOOK

What is lost when newspapers fold?

One standout service a newspaper provides, other than important news alerts and summaries — in addition to calendar and other items — is an opportunity for the scrapbook compiler.

How will scrapbooks be compiled if newspapers go dark?

For years, newspapers have come to be known as the source of "clippings." Those clippings could be recipes, wedding engagements, birth announcements, obituaries, high school and college sporting events, features of loved ones, and/or events that people hold near and dear to their hearts.

Amazon itself still sells newspaper scrapbooks. The hobby stores have shelves of them.

I remember speaking to a digital expert one time at the *Patriot-News* when I was a sales representative. We were selling *Central PA Magazine*, a glossy bimonthly publication, affiliated with the local PBS TV station, WITF. He was used to selling only digital delivery of ads: in other words, behavior-targeted ads for different businesses. His dilemma: he would often get requests from clients to PROVE those ads were delivered correctly. The clients can never see their ads (no wonder, since their client base doesn't include their own behavior, necessarily).

But the ad representative was mesmerized by the magazine. The millennial-generation representative, who didn't read magazines at all, was making a statement that if the half-page ad appears on page 32, that means the same ad is always on page 32 no matter where it is seen, no matter where the reader is finding the magazine. The representative thought that was amazing and great proof of delivery for an advertising client.

I said something to the effect of "no kidding." It's only worked for a couple of hundred years.

The reasoning always behind scrapbook-assembling is the same: what appeared in that edition of the newspaper most likely was seen or read by friends or neighbors. The chances they have seen it are a lot higher than catching a chance for potential delivery to friends/colleagues via social media. So the information is legitimate, for real. And newspapers that are collected and preserved by readers will have a greater sense of permanence compared to a social-media post.

For those who don't already know, when you post on social media, you do NOT reach all your friends. Trust me, Facebook and LinkedIn and Instagram are businesses and want you to PAY to reach everybody.

What are future scrapbooks going to look like without newspaper clippings? Printouts of social media posts?

If the newspaper industry is reduced to websites and digital push notifications, is that what scrapbooks in decades to come going to look like?

And what familiarity will a scrapbook addition have if people don't recognize it immediately, as they do when people paste the newspaper's nameplate and date over the article?

Newspapers give scrapbooks and history compilations real legitimacy because, like the story of Central PA Magazine, there is a feeling that thousands of people have (potentially) read the story, because it appeared in a newspaper that has thousands of readers, and here is the proof. A scrapbook is a living, breathing proof of history that is accessed time and again.

So woe to us if we lose newspapers, because we are losing any legitimacy with the stuff we display in scrapbooks.

My Role in It

I have spent time looking over my role in the magazine and newspaper field the past 40 years.

In the next 40 years, newspaper survival will depend entirely on news organization leadership.

If they follow the model I have outlined — producing hyper-local special sections geared for a readership that craves and demands information about their community, allowing all readers, and advertisers, a consistent voice and a platform — I think newspapers can not only survive, but thrive.

It's a lot more than covering the news. It is celebrating diversity and diverse opinions. It is actively looking for those views and opinions and showcasing them.

What does that leadership look like?

Forty years ago there was the editor-in-chief, or executive editor. They had true power. They were true leaders. Owners of newspapers put their faith and trust in them.

These days, middle managers and direct supervisors are given almost no power anymore. In the media field, direct supervisors have virtually no power. How can you lead when you are not given the power to make tough decisions? When your say over who to fire or hire does not exist? In the past, the editor-in-chief had all the power. These days they have almost none.

I think there can and should be a balanced approach with advertising and news departments. Neither "side" should feel detrimental to either. You can report the news and still make money. But it takes more work to develop specially themed and community-engaged sections. Still, fearless, well-researched, in-depth reporting should and can continue.

The responsibility rests on everyone involved in the industry, and particularly on advertising. When I worked for the Harrisburg *Patriot-News*, one sales manager told me that unless the creative is spectacular on an ad, and is just right, the ad would not work. Ads in newspaper are a showcase for what a company has. They are a tool to assist sales. That's what they are all about.

A longtime friend and good colleague of mine recently posted on Facebook about the battles he has against the trolls on his favorite social platform. My response to him was this:

In some instances, you have to choose your battles wisely. I have been the victim of my own stubborn insistence on winning non life-threatening battles. One of them is sticking with my own industry, newspapers, dying because of completely inept management and resistance to much-needed change. In a couple of cases, these have been self-inflicted wounds. I don't want to retire. Yet.

Items No More: The Buggy Whip

There was a time in which items once existed that are no more.

Take the buggy whip, for example. Before the horseless carriage, or automobile, was invented, there were slews of businesses in the country that made horse whips for the carriages that transported everybody. When automobiles were introduced at the beginning of the 20th century, there was no need for them.

In SucceedingInSmallBusiness.com, in 2015, Jeanne Yocum wrote:

When I lived in western Massachusetts, my town was just across the Connecticut River from Holyoke, which is known as "Paper City" because it was once one of the world's largest centers for paper manufacturing. A half hour away was Westfield, a town that carries the nickname "Whip City." During the 19th century, Westfield was a center for the manufacturing of buggy whips.

A whip manufacturer, Westfield Whip, still operates in Westfield. On their website they say they are the only survivor of the 42 whip manufacturers that operated there in the 19th century. They serve people who are involved in dressage and similar activities.

I'm not certain any paper is being manufactured in Holyoke today; if it is, it's certain to be of a specialty nature. Fortunately, after years of decline the city is making a comeback as a high tech center.

When did the owners of the companies that earned Holyoke its nickname begin to realize that two factors — rising labor costs and a rapidly dwindling stock of timber upstream that could be floated to their mills on the Connecticut River — would come together to move their industry to places with more abundant timber and labor cheaper?

Similarly, did the whip makers in Westfield realize when the first automobile drove into town that their companies were doomed? Or did they cling to the hope that most people would not want one of those noisy, newfangled contraptions?

Why bring up these bits of business history? Because I often wonder how much time, if any, the average small business owner devotes to scanning the environment for emerging factors that may affect the future of his/her business.

Over my career, I've worked at several companies that had to reinvent themselves to avoid being crushed by market shifts far beyond their control. One of these companies no longer exists; it was swallowed up by a larger, nimbler competitor that was better at judging the emerging needs of the marketplace. Another company's business looks dramatically different than it did when I was there, as they've sold off some business lines and acquired new ones.

In one case, a small public relations firm, the harbingers of doom were clear long before the owner took action to save the organization. The firm had as much as 80% of its client base in one industry, and a risky one at that — real estate. When the region's housing and commercial markets crashed in spectacular style in the late 1980s, it was a miracle the company survived. Yet, the signs that a crash was inevitable began to show up as least two years earlier. The handwriting was on the wall; the firm owner just chose to ignore it. A severe downsizing and some deep financial hurt for the owner followed before the ship was righted with a much more diverse client roster.

Yokum's advice:

Make sure you routinely take time to scan the horizon for developments that might affect your business' future, either negatively or positively. It is all too easy to just stay down in the trenches working day after day on short-term issues without ever standing up and taking a good look around for what might be coming next. Don't let that happen to you.

It's the same with typewriters, a precursor to our modern-day home computers, tablets and smartphones.

Before the internet, newspapers were essentially the whip. After the invention of the internet (automobile), whip manufacturing practically ceased.

In ThoughtCo.com, in 2019, contributor Mary Bellis wrote about the first typewriters:

Christopher Sholes was an American mechanical engineer, born on February 14, 1819, in Mooresburg, Pennsylvania, and died on February 17, 1890, in Milwaukee, Wisconsin. He invented the first practical modern typewriter in 1866, with the financial and technical support of his business partners Samuel Soule and Carlos Glidden. Five years, dozens of experiments, and two patents later, Sholes and his associates produced an improved model similar to today's typewriters.

The Sholes typewriter had a type-bar system and the universal keyboard was the machine's novelty, however, the keys jammed easily. To solve the jamming problem, another business associate, James Densmore, suggested splitting up keys for letters commonly used together to slow down typing. This became today's standard "QWERTY" keyboard.

Christopher Sholes lacked the patience required to market a new product and decided to sell the rights to the typewriter to James Densmore. He, in turn, convinced Philo Remington (the rifle manufacturer) to market the device. The first "Sholes & Glidden Typewriter" was offered for sale in 1874 but was not an instant success. A few years later, improvements made by Remington engineers gave the typewriter machine its market appeal and sales skyrocketed.

As early as the 1970s, word processors were invented that could be used at home.

From Mary Bellis in ThoughtCo.com in January 2020, this story explains the origins of word processing software:

Released in 1979 by Micropro International, WordStar was the first commercially successful word processing software program produced for microcomputers. It became the best-selling software program of the early 1980s.

Its inventors were Seymour Rubenstein and Rob Barnaby. Rubenstein had been the director of marketing for IMS Associates, Inc. (IMSAI). This was a California-based computer company, which he left in 1978 to start his own software company. He convinced Barnaby, the chief programmer for IMSAI, to join him. He gave Barnaby the task of writing a data processing program.

That was the beginning of the end for typewriters, although some writers still insist on using them to this day. One of my favorite authors, Harlan Ellison, stayed true to his craft — and his typewriter — until the day he died in 2018.

I read a lot of newspapers, including the *Reading Eagle*, the *Patriot-News* and *LNP*. I used to read the *New York Times*, religiously, every Sunday. I read the *Philadelphia Inquirer* when I can. I read several weeklies in my region as well: *The Hershey Sun, The Lititz Record-Express, The Community Courier* and even the *Hershey Merchandiser*.

I do that at my favorite table with my favorite cup of coffee.

Why I love the newspaper even to this day is the fact that is easily available, is self-contained, has more content than any website, and can be saved, stored and reread at any time. Newspapers serve as markers and conduits for our history, regionally and nationally. Nothing can replace the newspaper, though many websites have tried. I know how difficult it is to sell targeted ads on newspaper websites, because I have done that in the past: three years' worth of full-time work. So I understand the training and challenges needed to conduct successful campaigns online.

My week would be dire and awkwardly incomplete if I was not given a chance to page through a great newspaper. I never miss the chance.

A Life Without a Newspaper

I can't imagine a life without a newspaper.

For many, a newspaper provides life direction: what is happening in my community and world right now?

Who died? Who got engaged? Who is celebrating a marriage?

What happened during that exciting game last night, hours after I went to bed?

When I sit to enjoy my coffee in the morning, how can I get an accurate, filtered, researched and verified account of what has been happening?

What about that delicious, highly intoxicating scent of recycled newsprint with soybean ink that stirs my mind and imagination every time I take the newspaper from the plastic bag it is wrapped in?

What about the great carriers and how important it has been to recognize and reward them on their birthday or during the winter holidays?

In "A World Without Newspapers," written in 2015, HuffPost contributing writer Michael Rosenblum has this to say about a world dwindling away, losing its love affair with newspapers:

> *All the news that's fit to print....*
>
> *I am old.*
>
> *I am so old that I still like to start each morning with a printed, paper newspaper at breakfast.*
>
> *I could read the paper online, on my iPad or my phone, but there is something enormously satisfying about the physicality of the paper.*
>
> *I have the NY Times delivered to my home every morning.*
>
> *This morning's NY Times was noticeably thin.*

In fact, most of the NY Times delivered to my house have been noticeably thin. Thinner and thinner.

It isn't for lack of content. It is for lack of advertising.

Watching the NY Times waste away before my eyes, at my breakfast table, is like having a close relative who is slowly dying of some wasting-away disease. It's an incremental thing, but my God.. you have lost a lot of weight.

And, as with the relative, this can't go on forever.

This was not always the case with The NY Times. It was once thick and fat. The Sunday edition used to be massive. Whole forests were chopped down to create that thing. And it was as thick with advertising as Vogue magazine — maybe thicker.

But no more.

Now it has what used to be called 'The Consumption'.

And The Times is not alone. Time Magazine these days is now thinner than the staple that holds it together. It is also almost devoid of ads. Newsweek, of course, vanished last year.

I would say that within my lifetime I shall see the end of newspapers — or at least the printed, physical kind.

This will be too bad. At least for me. I suppose for a generation that grew up without having read a paper paper (so to speak), and I would assume this is pretty much everyone now under the age of 30, the loss will go almost unnoticed.

Kind of like the disappearance of the icebox. Or the horse and carriage. Or the typewriter (whatever that was).

It's the inevitable and irresistible consequence of technological progress.

Oh, I suppose there will be a few holdouts who cling to some simulacrum of a paper; and if there is a market, someone, somewhere will actually produce a printed paper — but these will be like the few who still insist that the only way to listen to recorded music is on vinyl.

Weirdos. Ummm. no... Interesting eccentrics.

And, no doubt, at some point in the not too distant future, a television network news program will do a piece on a small group of eccentrics who still 'read the newspaper on a piece of paper', and the small printing shop that feeds their desire.

That is, of course, assuming that there is still a network TV news show to watch.

And of that, I have my doubts.

How This Book Has Changed Me

Newspapers remain a critical part of our lives. They can change our behavior. They can lead our thoughts. We are sometimes brought to tears because of a good story. When we pick up a newspaper, we want to read about justice, about overcoming adversity, about surviving and thriving despite all odds.

Many of the lifestyle readers have scrapbooks brimming with newspaper articles. I have seen some of those collections by youth groups that were featured in publications at LNP Weeklies. I have been shown many newspaper clippings from the readers of the *Harrisburg Patriot-News* and *Reading Eagle.*

As I wrote this book, I relived the era of the late 1970s and early 1980s, when newspapers reigned supreme. I could resurrect, from memory, the "indicators" of those times. And nobody foresaw this future where newspapers and their staffs have somehow, someway been deemed nonessential.

The future looked bright for print journalists, and instead turned unbearably grim.

The future of newspapers is going to have to involve incredibly creative and suave management, and those executives have to love newspaper work. If you don't love it, then don't ruin the work of news organizations by being a non-participating, non-contributing part of it.

I was listening to a videoblog on LinkedIn one day by a colleague. It was a fairly simple presentation on what makes a good manager. I have seen few good managers as a newspaper employee.

Manager decisions to hire or fire can be based on pure pettiness, which I have seen far too often:

My answer to my video blog colleague was this:

Your presentation makes perfect sense. But I can't tell you how many times in my four-decade work history that I have seen pettiness, laziness and a couldn't-care-less attitude on the part of management. I have come to the conclusion that in this world, you are kept and well-managed if they like you. I think it just comes down to that: are you well-liked? I have seen far too many people lose a career opportunity because of petty bad blood between the manager and the worker. And how much does a manager want to invest in trying to help someone they just don't like?

AFTERWORD

You watch them often enough: one-on-one television interviews or a question-and-answer feature in the newspaper where the question comes up: Would you do it all over again?

Like a feature film script, I would have to write two separate endings.

One ending would talk about how wonderful it was while it lasted, writing and editing for four decades. I will choose to have nothing but positive comments to make, about how I was so grateful for the opportunity and I have plenty of wonderful memories of my time as a reporter and an editor.

I would reminisce about how great newspapers were when I entered the field. The sky was the limit.

I would thank all those who gave me the opportunity.

However, I am not likely to provide that scenario. I am a realist. I like to look over the chances I took and those I didn't and judge them. Repeatedly.

The more likely ending would involve one in which the harsh, uncontrollable realities of layoffs intrude on any dream memories. The incredible sinking feeling of uncertainty as, bit by bit, the industry eroded and was collapsed by online advertising and search. About the shrinking newsrooms. The incredible uncertainty of having a job. Of the periods I wasn't working and worrying about whether I would ever work again.

In between work in the late 1980s, I attended Millersville University in Millersville, Pennsylvania to complete my teaching degree and follow my father's certain and secure career path as a career teacher. I was tired of uncertainty. If I could have completed my education (sadly, I ran out of money), I could have begun as a writing instructor 30 years ago, with three months off for the year, plenty of benefits and a pension I could have cashed in by now.

If you believe in the verity of the cliché about "how, despite what I know, I would do it all again," unfortunately that's not me. Honestly, I have regrets that strain at me. I love the field and will stay in it. But there is one caveat:

If I would only have known about how uncertain the newspaper industry would become, I think I would have found some way to become a teacher. I would have missed a lot of joy by avoiding this field, but I would have avoided a lot of pain. I may have had to endure a different pain, but the pain that stays familiar is one in which most people yearn to part with.

What decision would you make?

Email me about your thoughts on this book at AndyAndrews@verizon.net. I would love to hear from you. I may want to post your comments in my ongoing social media sites.

And please, keep reading the newspaper

— Andy Andrews
December 2020

SHOUTOUTS

Cover by Suzy Rae Design (www.suzyraedesign.com).

Special thanks go to my wife Debbie, who read the initial draft and offered poignant criticisms and corrections; Jean Henshaw, who provided critical suggestions to improve the book; graphic design artist Suzy Rae Lysczek of Suzy Rae Design LLC, Reading, for the fantastic book cover; and my colleagues at Entrepreneurs Connection, PAK, Berks Elder Network, HealthNet, the Eastern Pennsylvania Business Owners Network, the Career Professional Executives Networking Group and countless others for their thoughts and inspiration.

CPSIA information can be obtained
at www.ICGtesting.com
Printed in the USA
BVHW012258050321
601896BV00010B/180

9 781953 710024